TOPICS IN TRANSLATION 4
Series Editors: Susan Bassnett (*University of Warwick*) and
André Lefevere (*University of Texas, Austin*)

The Coming Industry of Teletranslation

Overcoming Communication Barriers through Telecommunication

Minako O'Hagan

MULTILINGUAL MATTERS LTD
Clevedon • Philadelphia • Adelaide

Library of Congress Cataloging in Publication Data

O'Hagan, Minako
The Coming Industry of Teletranslation: Overcoming Communication Barriers
Through Telecommunication/Minako O'Hagan
Topics in Translation: 4
Includes bibliographical references and index.
1. Translating services. 2. Telecommunication. 3. Wide area networks (computer
networks). 4. Communication, international. 5. Translating and interpreting–
Technological innovations. 6. Machine translating. I. Title. II. Series.
P306.2.O37   1996
418'.02'0285–dc20   95-40682

British Library Cataloguing in Publication Data

A CIP catalogue record for this book is available from the British Library.

ISBN 1-85359-326-5 (hbk)
ISBN 1-85359-325-7 (pbk)

Multilingual Matters Ltd

UK: Frankfurt Lodge, Clevedon Hall, Victoria Road, Clevedon, Avon BS21 7SJ.
USA: 1900 Frost Road, Suite 101, Bristol, PA 19007, USA.
Australia: P.O. Box 6025, 83 Gilles Street, Adelaide, SA 5000, Australia.

Copyright © 1996 Minako O'Hagan

Typeset by Archetype, Stow-on-the-Wold.
Printed and bound in Great Britain by WBC Book Manufacturers Ltd.

NORWELL 1996

The Coming Industry of Teletranslation

TOPICS IN TRANSLATION

Series Editors: Susan Bassnett (*University of Warwick*)
and André Lefevere (*University of Texas, Austin*)

Editor for Annotated Texts for Translation: Beverly Adab (*Aston University, Birmingham*)

Editor for Translation in the Commercial Environment:
Geoffrey Samuelsson-Brown (*Aardvark Translation Services Ltd*)

Other Books in the Series

Annotated Texts for Translation: French – English
    BEVERLY ADAB
Annotated Texts for Translation: English – French
    BEVERLY ADAB
Linguistic Auditing
    NIGEL REEVES and COLIN WRIGHT
Paragraphs on Translation
    PETER NEWMARK
Practical Guide for Translators
    GEOFFREY SAMUELSSON-BROWN
Translation, Power, Subversion
    R. ALVAREZ and M. C.-A. VIDAL (eds)

Other Books of Interest

About Translation
    PETER NEWMARK
Cultural Functions of Translation
    C. SCHÄFFNER and H. KELLY-HOLMES (eds)
Mission Incomprehensible: The Linguistic Barrier to Effective Police Co-operation in Europe
    ROY D. INGLETON

Please contact us for the latest book information:
Multilingual Matters Ltd, Frankfurt Lodge, Clevedon Hall,
Victoria Road, Clevedon, Avon, England, BS21 7SJ.

Contents

Foreword

This book addresses what is about to become one of the great challenges and opportunities of the emerging information society – the need for, and the development of, a global teletranslation industry.

The peoples of Europe now cross with ease the borders they have fought over for millennia. The North American Free Trade Agreement means that English, Spanish, Portuguese and French speakers need to work with each other the length and breadth of the Americas. The Pacific Economic Co-operation Committee Triple T Project forecasts vast growth in tourism, transport and telecommunications and that by 2010 two hundred and fifty million people will cross the Pacific annually and it will be possible to fly from London to Tokyo in two hours. Even the vast Pacific ceases to be a barrier separating the cultures that rim it. But as it becomes easier for people who speak different languages to intermingle by travel or telecommunications, and as more of them do so, how do they communicate in a way that promotes greater understanding? This is the issue that faces the translation industry.

Koji Kobayashi, in his vision of an information society, said: 'At present people can talk between the major cities of the world at any time by directly dialling the number of the other party. However, such a development in international communication capabilities has yet to produce sufficiently mutual understanding among nations in today's world. One of the major obstacles is the difference in languages from nation-to-nation.' To overcome this problem, Koji Kobayashi proposed the development of an automatic interpretation telephone system as a component of a global communications system. He said this would come into existence by the end of the millennium. The technology depends upon developments in a branch of computer technology called 'machine translation' which Minako O'Hagan describes in Chapter 2, and a new generation of telecommunications which she describes in Chapter 3.

Another technology that will be in place by the end of the 1990s is a network of Low Earth Orbiting Satellites (LEOS). These hold the promise that no matter where a person is, or whether there is a conventional terrestrial telecommunication infrastructure, they can be linked into a global information network using a mobile phone into which they can plug a laptop computer. If it is then also possible to call on an automatic interpretation service, do we not have a solution to the world's communication problems?

Minako O'Hagan, in her prologue says: 'Now that we are solving the technical problems, the real problem of communication is emerging and it is formidable.' The marriage of artificial intelligence and super highways of information that is represented in the idea of an automatic interpretation telephone service may provide touch of the button, anywhere, anytime, translation, but the meaning in such translation is only denotative. This may be adequate for communicating of a strictly scientific, quantitative or impersonal nature, but most communication carries a second level of connotative meaning that comes from culture, context and the subtle swirls of meaning that lie in a tone of voice, the grip of a handshake, the degree of a bow, the clothes that are worn and the selection of site for a meeting. Taking these factors into account requires skilled human translators. It is Minako O'Hagan's insight to recognise the implications for the developing technologies of translation of the difference between denotative and connotative translation. She looks at how new telecommunication technologies will be used to mobilise networks of specialist translators, and in Chapter 4 describes the development of the teletranslation industry as a balanced use of human and machine translation.

This book is visionary in the way it looks at the emergence of a new information industry as a support service for the information society. It is also, however, eminently practical and provides in Chapter 5 a road map for a teletranslation service. It deserves careful reading by those who are directly involved in the translation industry and want to know where it is going. It also merits wider attention. As the global information society takes shape, every aspect of society will find itself increasingly involved with issues that involve translation.

John W. Tiffin
David Beattie Professor of Communication
Victoria University of Wellington

Acknowledgements

In writing this book, I received assistance from various sources. I am grateful to the Telecommunications Users Association of New Zealand (TUANZ) and Telecom New Zealand Ltd for their research grants. Their financial assistance enabled me to visit AT&T Language Line (US), Translatel (France), ITU Interpreting Service (Switzerland), KDD Teleserve (Japan), Advanced Telecommunications Research Institute International (ATR) (Japan), Japan Electronic Industry Development Association (JEIDA), The University of Manchester Institute of Science and Technology (UMIST) (UK), and the Institute of Translation and Interpreting (UK).

In addition to the helpful information given by people I met in person in the above organisations, the assistance provided in cyberspace has been invaluable. I often discovered an unexpected symbiosis shared by translators all over the world expressed in the 'honyaku' Internet Mailing List discussion group which gave me a sense of assurance that we all face similar problems working as translators and interpreters irrespective of location.

I am also indebted to my academic supervisor, Professor Tiffin of the Victoria University of Wellington, for his encouragement and guidance throughout this project. Lastly, but not least, I am grateful for the assistance given by Dr John Jamieson, polyglot extraordinaire, for his input as a professional translator.

Prologue

While the printer is spitting out a copious report just translated into Spanish, the translator's mind is already on another job which should at any moment be delivered via modem – his translation of a financial document previously sent to a subject expert in Sydney for fine tuning. This is a standard procedure for such a highly specialised translation before final delivery of the job to the local Greek client. Meanwhile a fax message arrives from a freelance translator working remotely from her seaside holiday cottage; it seeks clarification of the meaning of one paragraph in the text she is translating into German. Immediately, another fax comes through; an urgent request for translation into Chinese of a 30-page contract to be used in Taiwan. A local native Chinese translator contacted by phone is unable to accept the job, but fortunately a translator in Singapore agrees to do the work. At the next desk an Arabic interpreter is engaged on an interpreting assignment by phone, assisting an American businessman to negotiate a deal with his Saudi client. She is in the middle of a three-way conference call, relaying the conversations in each language.

This glimpse into a modern translation office in Auckland, New Zealand, demonstrates how information technology (IT) has not only penetrated but become a lifeline for the language business in a relatively short time. The era of electric typewriters was replaced by wordprocessors in the 1980s and the latter progressively expanded to include a wide range of languages. Then multilingual desktop publishing (DTP) became a reality with electronic typesetting equipment producing camera-ready copy which can be sent directly to a printer to produce a top quality publication. At the same time, impressive progress in telecommunications technology also contributed to the transformation of the translation business. It expanded the translation market into the international arena, initially through the use of fax machines alone and then increasingly through modem communications. It also widened the human resource pool via networking from remote locations – translation work does not have to be done in the office or even within the country as long as budget and deadline requirements are met. As a result, during the past decade the translation business has grown from a metropolitan service into an international business, thanks largely to IT.

Working in the translation industry over the past decade, I have witnessed these changes first hand. But there have been equally significant changes in the nature of the demand for language services. I have observed these in three main areas.

Firstly, a decade ago language needs were greatly underestimated by the business community. A lack of sensitivity to language barriers and a low awareness of their negative influence on business prevailed, particularly in English-speaking countries which had historically enjoyed the status of speakers of the lingua franca of the world. Non-English speakers were generally expected to use English when it came to international business communication. Recently, however, lowering trade barriers between domestic and world markets and the related increase in competition have led to a change in attitude in the business community with a realisation that one has to adopt the customer's language in order to compete successfully. Simultaneously, a general increase in information acquisition and distribution efforts in an attempt to gain a competitive edge has boosted demand for the translation of articles from technical/trade journals, newsletters, patents, regulations, PR materials and product catalogues – to name but a few.

The changing nature and increasing volume of translation work being undertaken seems to me to signal that McLuhan's 'global village' is finally becoming a reality. Businesses are expanding their markets across national boundaries into culturally and linguistically foreign territory. Furthermore, and this is the second major area of change, it is becoming more likely for individuals to be involved in cross-cultural communication. Immigration, cultural/educational exchanges, direct broadcast satellite news, and tourism are but a few examples of increasing 'globalization', a term defined by Peter Robinson (1991), a senior telecommunications researcher, as 'the process of expanding cross-border linkages in a wider and growing variety of social, cultural, political, business, economic and legal areas. They are occurring at all levels of society'. This process, which is well under way, is boosting demand for language services. Interpreters and translators whose customers were, until recently limited to multinational corporations, government agencies and academics, now serve a much wider spectrum of clients.

The third factor to impact on language needs – the most important and unprecedented phenomenon in my opinion – is a development which lies behind physical movements of money, goods and people. It is the electronic movement of information in the form of data, voice and image via telecommunications links. In this world of interlinked computers, sometimes called 'cyberspace', an enormous amount of cross-cultural communication is taking place. This realm of communication has already had a major influence on many sectors of the service industry, but its ultimate impact will be revolutionary. The translation industry is going to be transformed.

The significance of telecommunications to the language business is simply that when people are connected electronically beyond country or cultural borders, be it via telephone, fax, electronic mail (e-mail) or visual images, they suddenly face a thick communication barrier – language. At this point all the modern technology becomes useless because the focal point shifts from the medium to the message of the communication. How can a monolingual Japanese businessman make himself understood to his Swedish counterpart when the two have no common language although their lines are connected? Is it always easy to organise translation when a handwritten message in Chinese arrives unexpectedly at the fax machine of an Italian shoe manufacturer? How do American researchers cope when they finally gain access via a workstation to the latest information on their target subject, only to find the report is in German? When your PC provides a gateway to a database, how will you understand the instructions on screen in a foreign language? Teleshopping, on-line entertainment and telelearning are coming your way very rapidly, but will they be offered in your language?

Put simply, the issue is: now that we are solving the technical problems, the real problem of communication is emerging and it is formidable. Different languages lie in wait as the stumbling block at the other end of the electronic highway, fully exposing the problematical nature of cross-cultural communication.

The *New York Times* reported in 1989 that the 'majority of documents and communications whose translation may be of significant benefit go untranslated due to the high cost and unavoidable delays of human manual translation' (Nirenburg *et al.*, 1992: 1). This accurately reflects the gap between supply and demand in the translation industry in the 1990s. Customers are often frustrated at the lengthy delays involved in translation and the correspondingly high prices. On the supply side, the increased demand has accentuated the shortage of human resources. Furthermore, the increased speed at which information can be transmitted means that customers insist on translation speeds to match. These challenges have driven the translation businesses to find ways to produce translation more efficiently. Technological solutions have been sought; faster computers, more efficient wordprocessing packages, access to multilingual terminology databases, increasing numbers of remotely located translators supporting the workload via fax and modem, and a revived interest in computerised automatic translation systems, Machine Translation (MT). But the bottom line is that translation is knowledge-intensive work which precludes easy automation and requires the expertise of well-trained professionals. Meanwhile, people are increasingly adopting the new communications environment such as the Internet, e-mail and video conferencing, and this in turn boosts demand for language services. Indications are that the gap between the supply and demand will widen further and this will inevitably have a retarding effect on the globalisation process. This leaves us with the big question: how are we going to cope with the ever increasing language problem?

This is why it is now time for us to rethink the whole business of translation. This book establishes how our needs to overcome language barriers are linked to the emergence of a new communications environment. It explores how such needs can be turned into one of the biggest business opportunities of the next century. The communication revolution will not be complete until the solution to the language issue is found. The marriage between language services and telecommunications technology holds the key.

1 Communications Technology and the Language Problem

March 1989, an international hotel in Auckland, New Zealand. A Japanese businessman with very limited English is experiencing some frustration on the phone. As he doesn't know the correct number to dial he calls the hotel reception. The English-speaking receptionist can't understand her Japanese guest, but assumes he wants to make an international call to Japan. She connects him with the international operator. The operator also has difficulty communicating with him, but is able to determine that he is Japanese and puts him through to an international operator in Japan. There is a brief conversation in Japanese. The bilingual Japanese operator passes a message to the New Zealand operator who then informs the hotel reception that the man would like to order breakfast delivered to his room.

This is the reality of the communication gap still prevalent and unresolved in the 20th century. The experience is not unique to New Zealand; this could be anywhere in the world. The primitive communication problem portrayed is in astonishing contrast with the sophistication of today's state of the art communications technology. While an American businessman can carry in his briefcase a notebook computer and a cellular phone, and convert a hotel room into a virtual office, he is totally helpless when modern telecommunications brings his Saudi client on the other end of the line, speaking Arabic, or when his urgent fax to Thailand fails to produce results. All this is because communications technology has done nothing to resolve the language barriers that prevent a free flow of communication among people who speak different languages. Indeed, it could be said that the advances of communications technology have exacerbated the problem.

1

The Information Superhighway and the Language Problem

Throughout much of today's world modern technology provides telecommunication links between people in ways that effectively mean that distance, time and quality have ceased to be an issue. We take it for granted that we can pick up a telephone and speak to someone on the other side of the world as easily and clearly as we can call across town. What makes this possible are webs of communications networks covering the globe, criss-crossing each other with electronic highways on which voice, data and images flow at the speed of light, oblivious to physical boundaries and national borders. These highways provide the backbone of the information infrastructure in the same way as the transport network provides the backbone of the physical infrastructure (Dordick, 1987: 22).

Computer technology plays a critical role in this information infrastructure. Computers not only form an integral part of all modern telecommunications systems, providing the 'intelligence' required to connect people on demand, they are increasingly 'customers' of telecommunications too, using the networks to link up to other computers in diverse geographical locations. Transferring data to a computer on the other side of the world is now almost as easy as making a telephone call to a neighbour. The term cyberspace, coined by William Gibson (1984) in his scientific fiction *Neuromancer*, is now commonly used to describe this 'world' of interlinked computers whereby information of any type is carried almost instantaneously in the form of digital signals over great distances. Its applications are many and varied. In cyberspace, the world's money markets are linked to one another, facilitating currency trading in real-time on a global basis, so that a change in the value of the Yen in London is immediately reflected on the Hong Kong market; airline, hotel and rental car reservation systems enable international travel arrangements to be made anywhere in the world from a travel agent's terminal; a university researcher can access a virtual library of millions of volumes and many thousands of papers in databases the world over. The growing use of personal computers at home has popularised electronic services such as bulletin board systems (BBS), and there is increasing interest in home banking, teleshopping and electronic mail (e-mail). In short, cyberspace provides the medium for the vast amounts of information required by commerce, industry, governments and the public. This experience has 'powerfully reinforced the collective imagination of computer users that there was another "world", a world where much of their social intercourse might take place, where much of their information would come from' (Woolley, 1992: 135) and is a perfect illustration of the nature and function of cyberspace.

The merging of computers with telecommunications technology has led to an increasingly porous and interlinked world, and is a major factor in the so-called globalisation process of growing interdependence among nation states which is arising from the expansion of cross-border linkages (Robinson, 1991). On the surface, these trends suggest a breaking down of barriers and an ongoing reduction, perhaps eventually even the elimination, of impediments to global communication. The reality, however, is not so straightforward. Growing international trade links mean that people will have to communicate with foreign business partners in other than their native language. Increasing use of the telephone as a sales and marketing tool will connect customers and suppliers from different cultures who use different languages. The ease of access to computer databases will mean that any information requested will be delivered, and almost instantaneously, but often in a language which the recipient may not understand.

The new information superhighways open the way to an enormous volume of cross-cultural communication, yet there are a variety of potential problems lurking within these electronic encounters. Perhaps some specific scenarios will demonstrate the point.

- Suppose you see a product advertised in a trade journal and it is just what you are looking for. The supplier is in Japan. You send off an enquiry by fax, asking for information urgently. A few days go by with no reply, so at the end of the week, you try telephoning. The call is answered in Japanese, a language you can't speak. After trying in vain to make yourself understood, you give up and prepare another fax message. Two weeks later, just when you had given up hope, out of the blue comes a reply by fax. It explains, in English, that it took them some time to get your message translated into Japanese and theirs into English. You wonder why they bother advertising the product in an English language journal.
- Even if you have an English-speaking business contact overseas, there is no guarantee that you can reach that particular person when you want to. Say you receive an urgent request for one of your products from a prospective client and you have to place a special order for materials with your supplier in China. You phone, but the call is answered by a non-English speaking secretary. Your desperate attempts to communicate fail so you give up and resort to the fax machine. But when you dial you hear a recorded message saying something completely unintelligible in Chinese, and the fax does not go through. You wonder if perhaps the number has changed, or is there congestion in the telephone network? By the time you finally

get hold of your English speaking contact a few days later it is too late
to place the order.

- Perhaps your business wants to advertise its toll-free '800' number in
  the international editions of a magazine. You're going to have to cope
  with enquiries from all over the world, and that is likely to mean
  enquiries in foreign languages.
- If you provide information and entertainment services, chat lines,
  help lines, etc. using '900' phone numbers where the charge for the
  information is added to the telephone account, have you considered
  the potential overseas market? With per minute international telephone charges now often less than the charge made for the information, it makes sense to market these services internationally, which
  again means catering for multiple languages.
- Suppose you use the Internet to tap into a source of information on
  your research topic, only to find that the content of the file transferred
  to you is in German, and you do not understand German.

In the past, distance and the lack of a sophisticated telecommunications
infrastructure acted to block cross-cultural communication. At the same
time this worked as a kind of buffer, sheltering people from the reality of
the language gap. There were fewer opportunities for people who lived
geographically far apart to come into contact. And even if they finally did
encounter one another their long journey might have prepared them
psychologically to expect different cultural conditions. They may even
have had time to learn something of the language. Similarly, written
correspondence took days or weeks to reach its destination and a few more
days having the document translated, if necessary, hardly affected the
overall time frame of the communication process. It seems that in the past
the difficulty of gaining communications access almost overrode the issue
of language problems. Although the actual language barrier is not any
greater now, the perceived barrier is, because of the ease of communication
access afforded by advancement of technology. Figure 1.1 illustrates that
while the impediments of cost, poor quality and distance have declined
over time with the implementation of technology, the language barrier has
remained the same, thus acquiring relatively greater significance.

The ease of international telecommunications is convincing us that
McLuhan's prediction of a converging world is now taking shape. As he
wrote in *The Gutenberg Galaxy*: 'The new electronic interdependence
recreates the world in the image of a global village' (1967: 31). But,
ironically, now that the technical problems are being solved the real
problem of communication is emerging, and it is immense. When the
extended information superhighway provides sophisticated pipelines to

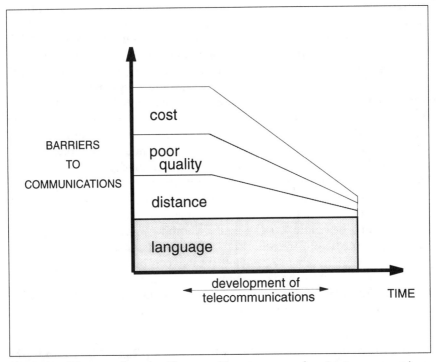

Figure 1.1 The growing significance of language as a barrier to communications

carry information, the users of the pipelines will be increasingly exposed to foreign language markets and cultures. Breaking this last barrier to communications is going to be a tough but interesting challenge.

Expanding Communications Horizons

But who is likely to be affected by language problems? First there are the international business people with markets covering the globe, the diplomatic and government officials and perhaps some fortunate well-funded scientists and academics. These groups are clearly major users of international telecommunications; but an important trend now emerging is that cross-cultural communication is increasingly touching the lives of ordinary citizens.

To understand how and why this will occur, it is helpful to look at the process of how telecommunications technology has progressively expanded our communication zone. It is not so very long ago that a phone call to another city was made only in special circumstances, and even then how nervously we watched the time tick by, clocking up expensive toll charges. High cost, poor quality transmission and the operator's voice all characterised long-distance calls. Today, because of reduced charges, increased quality and ease of access, we use the telephone just to have a casual chat, talking to someone in the same street or on the other side of the world with equal ease. Furthermore you don't have to be beside your phone at home or the office to make a call; you can carry a mobile telephone and stay in touch while moving from place to place, and answer-phones and voice mail take messages while you are out. You can divert your incoming calls to any numbers you specify even outside the country. What is more, today's telecommunications convey not only voice, but data and images as well. Fax machines deliver your written messages instantly, regardless of location, and the whole process involves nothing more than feeding in the document and dialling the number. Using modems, you can send data from your computer directly to a remotely located computer over the telephone line in a matter of seconds. Videophones are starting to appear on the market with video conferencing capturing business interest. Most of these activities will at least sound familiar to you, even if they have not already entered your life.

With advances in telecommunications technology we have now expanded our communication zones from intra-city to the whole country and beyond, to the international horizon. Until recently international calls for residential telephone subscribers were a rarity, but the situation is changing rapidly. Nowadays the busiest periods for Telecom New Zealand's international telephone exchanges are typically on Mother's Day and Christmas Day; these are social, not business calls. For computer aficionados, another example is the recent proliferation of BBS whereby electronic messages are exchanged between computers throughout the country and beyond. In May 1993 it was reported (Elmer-Dewitt, 1993) that 'the number of small computer-bulletin-board systems in America has jumped from 30,000 last year to more than 46,000 this year'. As of August 1993 the giant international 'network of computer networks', Internet, comprised 15,160 different networks supporting at least 1,776,000 host computers in 60 countries. This is a gigantic leap from 213 computers which participated in the Internet in 1981 (Obenaus, 1993). The actual number of end-users was estimated to be 25 million in 1994 and is doubling every year (Elmer-Dewitt, 1994). Furthermore, developing economies are placing a strong emphasis on expanding both their domestic telecommunications networks and their links with the rest of the world. Why? Because they are anticipating a great

demand for international communication and realise the adverse consequences of lagging behind in telecommunications infrastructure.

This progressive interconnection among countries is resulting in a
significant change in our communication behaviour. As the technology
forges connectivity beyond national borders and makes international
communication affordable, our way of thinking is shifting from a 'national'
framework to a 'global' perspective just as we moved our communication
zone from 'local' to 'national' when, for example, consumers began to think
of availability of goods not in terms of the stock in a local shop, but in a
nation-wide chain of shops and when more and more companies began
advertising single nation-wide toll-free phone numbers instead of separate
local numbers in each city. Soon we will be thinking in terms of
international chains of shops. In fact, with easy access to foreign advertising
in magazines and satellite TV this has already become a reality for many;
we can directly order books, for example, by fax and sometimes by e-mail
from an overseas publisher, bypassing the local book store. Many internationally linked businesses today have adopted this 'global' thinking, and
now the impact is reaching the individual consumer level.

These are just a few examples of how communications technology is
impacting on our lives in a significant way. Technologies and services that
were rare, expensive and quite out of reach just a few years ago are now
commonplace throughout the developed world, and national communications systems are rapidly being linked to provide connectivity between an
increasing proportion of the world's population. One of the most tangible
ways to measure this factor and the extent to which international
telecommunications is now a reality is the measured volume of calls.
Japan's Ministry of Posts and Telecommunications estimated that in 1993
over 2.3 billion minutes were spent on international telephone calls in Japan
(New Breeze, 1995), up 10% on the previous year, and statistics for Telecom
New Zealand show that in the year to March 1995 its callers originated 38.6
million international calls, up 19.9% on 1994 figures (Telecom Corporation
of New Zealand Limited 1995 Annual Report, 1995: 1).

In fact, most countries throughout the world have experienced unprecedented growth in international telecommunications traffic in recent years,
and forecast continued growth with falling costs. However, what the
statistics cannot reveal is how much time callers waste trying to break
through language barriers, the costs of the resulting misunderstandings, or
the suppressed demand due to anticipated problems with language, which
make people give up before they even try to make an international call. The
indications are, though, that the growing accessibility to, and use of,

telecommunications technology will mean that increasing numbers of people will need to be 'connected' across language and cultural barriers, for a variety of reasons. With several thousand languages currently spoken in the world, of which about 50 are in significant use, there will inevitably be more electronic encounters between people who lack a common language.

In the 1960s, Marshall McLuhan's 'the medium is the message' concept provided an insight into how communications media affect the messages they carry. But this presupposed that the content of the message is meaningful to the recipient once delivered. From a cultural and linguistic perspective in a world of advanced telecommunications, this premise is challenged; the medium is increasingly transparent and we are now facing a post-McLuhan stage where the importance of message content is superseding that of the medium. Regardless of the speed and accuracy of transmission, if the content of the message is not meaningful to the recipient because it remains locked into a foreign language paradigm, then the communication has effectively failed.

Translation Market – Past, Present and Future

The standard means of overcoming a language barrier has been to use language services offered by translators (of the written word) and interpreters (of the spoken word). Language services are not a newly established business sector. In fact, the circumstances demanding language assistance were clearly recognised long before the current information explosion and accompanying globalisation process. When communication difficulties were anticipated due to the absence of a common language between the sender and the recipient of a message, translators or interpreters were commonly called upon to bridge the gap. For example, at world trade negotiation talks between government officials, an inter-preter would be arranged to facilitate the communication; international conferences would often engage a team of interpreters and translators; the scientific and academic communities would routinely call for translations of abstracts, academic papers, patents, etc. These assignments continue to be a good source of business for language service operators today.

Within the needs described above it is only fair to point out that non-English speaking nations have historically made considerably more effort to break language barriers by conforming to English than the other way around. This is based on a widespread acceptance of English as the lingua franca of the world. As Steiner (1992) comments in his book *After Babel*: 'Science, technology, commerce and world finance speak more or less American English… Computers and data-banks chatter in "dialects" of an

Anglo-American mother tongue.' According to survey results published by JEIDA (Japan Electronic Industry Development Association), 84.4% of total translations undertaken in Japan in 1991 were between Japanese and English. But the over-reliance on English has had its drawbacks in the globalised marketplace, by engendering complacency, as illustrated in an Australian report (Valverde, 1990: 2) commissioned by the Office of Multicultural Affairs, Department of the Prime Minister and Cabinet, in 1990: 'The learning of languages other than English has always been left to others and English speakers seem to believe that everybody has to learn their language, even their clients. They seem to ignore the well-known trading axiom that "you buy in your language but you sell in the language of your customers".'

The *New York Times* estimated that the world market for translations was at least US$20 billion in 1989 and growing at the rate of 20% annually (Nirenburg *et al.*, 1992: 11). A special 'Translation Business' issue of the *Japan Times* (August 1992) reported that in 1991 the Japanese domestic market alone generated translations worth around 60 billion yen, not counting in-house translations undertaken by major corporations. According to the Japan Translation Federation (Sakamoto & Itagaki, 1993), Japan's annual translation market is in excess of 1 trillion yen. In the UK, the demand for translation services has risen by more than 50% during the past five years with British companies spending over £50 million in 1992 on translations aiming at Europe and other world markets for their products and services (Newmark, 1993: 137).

Within these macro trends, micro trends are emerging as a direct impact of technology applications. In the past the demand pattern for language services tended to be reasonably well-defined and predictable and as a result supply and demand seemed more or less in balance. In today's information-hungry society, however, needs are changing in a number of ways. A major new requirement of language services is speed. Clients need to be able to quickly select the important material out of huge volumes of superfluous information and to disseminate the information rapidly in a given language. The time frames for translations are shrinking to a level comparable with the speed of information exchange made possible by IT. Professor Sager (1990) of the Centre for Computational Linguistics, Manchester, UK, addressing the 10th Anniversary of Translating and the Computer conference, pointed out that the inherent delays incurred as a result of human-based translation will no longer be acceptable because of their negative influence on the otherwise free flow of information afforded by information technology. For example, as manufacturing processes become faster and product lives generally shorter, multilingual products have to follow the same short time frames. The value of information will increasingly rely on its 'newness'.

Related to the speed factor is an expectation by language service users of a smooth interface between their particular communications environment and that of the language service provider. Inflexible paper-based translation services or interpreting limited to face-to-face settings requiring plenty of advance notice are simply no longer sufficient in a world of electronic information exchange and tele-conferences. Many new circumstances requiring language assistance are emerging. International telephone-based services, on-line database access, and the entertainment provided via Direct Broadcast Satellite TV programmes, for example, can each bring requirements for translation or interpreting. Again, the speed factor is important. For example, instead of being prepared to wait a few days for the translation of patent details gathered from an on-line database, a scientist will need the information in his own language in a matter of hours, otherwise the benefit of on-line access would be lost. The translated minutes of a video conference may well be required immediately after the session concludes. Finally, clients' expectations about the price of language services are changing in a complex manner: on the one hand, the process of 'unlocking' the information buried in an unknown language is increasingly valued, making translators' and interpreters' contributions more appreciated. On the other hand, falling prices for telecommunications and access to information together with growing availability of 'cheap options' for translation using Machine Translation (MT) based products, mean users may expect to pay less for fully fledged professional interpreting and translation services.

In summary, the language business is faced with the major challenges of achieving much greater throughput, shorter production time frames and consistent quality at low cost while providing easy access and smooth integration of their services into their user's communications environment. The realisation of instantaneous global telecommunications will expand users' expectations on communication beyond 'anywhere', 'at any time' and 'via any medium' to include 'any language'. Achieving this will necessitate significant changes to today's language services.

Technology Applications: Benefits and Limitations

Due to IT and the resulting information revolution, the language service industry has already undergone a huge change in the past decade. A new set of 'language technology' computer applications has streamlined the text generation process; the paper dictionary and typewriter-based translation offices of the 1980s now use multilingual wordprocessing with spell checkers and grammar/style checkers, on-line foreign terminology data-bases, CD-ROM dictionaries, and DTP systems to add value to the raw translation of texts. The use of telecommunications technology has also had a significant impact. Fax machines have made translation businesses to a large extent location-independent and able to offer their services internationally. Also, translation companies which have traditionally augmented their in-house staff with freelance translators on a job-to-job basis are now finding remote working via telecommunications is an ideal way to do this. These outside translators are increasingly using modems to link their computers to the telephone network, which allows them to receive and send their work in real-time from screen to screen, improving production efficiency and expanding translation companies' resources even across national borders. The fact that a significant propor-tion of the members of the Institute of Translation and Interpreting (ITI) of the UK reside outside the country may reflect the heavy use of communi-cations technology.

But despite these advancements there are still a number of unresolved technical issues, such as the electronic transmission of multilingual texts encoded using non-ASCII character sets and incompatibility between different wordprocessing software packages. A more fundamental prob-lem lies in the fact that most of the new technologies are merely tools used by human experts and as long as human translators remain an essential element in the language translation process, they will also act as a bottleneck. This is the reason behind the revived interest shown in MT or computer-based automatic translation systems in recent years. MT is a computer application which uses software programs to convert one written natural language into another. It sounds like an ideal solution – a way to overcome the human factor and break the language barrier once and for all. And yet, in reality the translation process is still largely a manual one for the fundamental reason that current MT technology cannot match many attributes of its human counterpart. However, it would be quite wrong to dismiss the potential capability of MT. Research is advancing steadily and already niche applications of MT are becoming popular. Indications are that human translators will increasingly be co-working with MT while a range of new applications will be developed in which MT will exceed the capabilities of human translators.

Telecommunications – A Solution to Language Issues?

Despite its critical importance, the language problem has so far received much less publicity than the technological leaps which are realising faster and cheaper communications. Also, the impact of language issues on the information revolution has been largely underestimated. This is partly due to the fact that much of the revolution has centred around the English language paradigm, which has reinforced the notion of English as the lingua franca of international communication. But this premise is now being shaken as our constantly expanding communication zones look set to take us deeper into foreign language territory.

Fortunately some telecommunications service providers have begun to recognise language issues as an impediment to the use of their services, and are addressing the problem in a number of ways. Perhaps the first, and yet not so obvious, example is the progressive implementation of international direct dialling. What a difference it made to tourists to be able to avoid the frustration of negotiating with a telephone operator in a foreign language every time they wanted to call home. But this did not solve the problem for calls such as 'collect' that still require an operator, so more recently the phone companies invented 'Home Country Direct' services which enable away from home callers to direct dial an operator back in their own country, avoiding the need to talk to a local operator in a foreign language. These facilities undoubtedly help to alleviate some of the language problems encountered by travellers, but they bypass rather than address the question of language barriers in telecommunications.

Some leading telecommunications companies have even entered the language translation market directly. Major telephone companies in the USA, France and Japan, for example, have each established subsidiaries specifically to cater for language needs. According to one such company, KDD Teleserve, its real-time telephone interpreting services provided by human interpreters have shown nearly a six-fold growth since its start of the operation in 1986, with 13,600 requests handled during the 1993 financial year.

The symbiotic links between telecommunications and language services have also been recognised by some computer network service operators. MT-based on-line translation services are now offered by several publicly accessible computer networks. Subscribers can select 'translation service' from a menu on their desktop terminal, send in the text and receive the finished translation via e-mail. Despite the varying quality of the MT output, some of these services are proving popular and are reported to be on the point of becoming commercially viable. At the same time, some of the world's major telephone companies are engaged in long-term R&D into automatic speech-to-speech translation with a view to developing a computer-based interpreting telephony system. Their aim is ultimately to enable telephone calls between speakers of different languages, assisted by computer to interpret the dialogue automatically into the required languages.

Teletranslation Service

In the opening anecdote,telecommunications came to the rescue of one customer faced with an intractable language problem, but they solved his problem almost by accident and in a rather unbusiness-like fashion. Telecommunications could, in future, play an important and much more structured and efficient role in the provision of language interpreting and translation services if inextricable linkages between telecommunications and language services were cultivated.

'Teletranslation' is the term I use to describe the offspring of the forthcoming marriage of these two previously unrelated branches of communication. Teletranslation will exploit the global networking capabilities of telecommunications technology to bring language service providers (using both human and computer resources) and their customers together. In doing so, it will help overcome many otherwise insoluble language problems.

In expanding on the issues touched upon in this chapter the remainder of the book depicts the important role teletranslation could play in your future, whether you are a provider or a user of language services, or just interested in the development of communications technologies and how they relate to language issues.

2 The Translation Business and the Impact of MT

... More than half the cost of international business is used up in dialogues of the deaf, between people who are totally ignorant of each other's laws, customs and business dialect.

The Ringmaster, (West, 1992: 9)

Language barriers are a fact of life and yet the cost of ignoring them is not always understood. As the world becomes progressively interlinked, the role of interlingual communication grows increasingly important and failure to recognise this can contribute as much friction to political, business and trade negotiations between countries as can more tangible issues such as balance sheet figures. Endymion Wilkinson (1983), an academic and EC diplomat who had postings in Japan, spelled out in his book *Japan versus Europe: A History of Misunderstanding* how trade friction stemmed from misunderstanding and that one major source of this was undoubtedly language difficulties. The same point is illustrated in this statement by an American observer (Smith, 1987): 'American politicians too frequently court disaster by relying on foreign leaders' English or their translations. Linguistic ineptitude can lead to serious misunderstandings.... ' At their worst, a language barrier can be a matter of life or death, as sadly demonstrated by an incident in 1992 in Louisiana. A Japanese student in disguise for Halloween was shot dead after moving despite a warning to 'freeze'. The victim, unfamiliar with colloquial English, hadn't understood what the word meant.

Paradoxically, advances in communications technology have tended to highlight the communication gap between different peoples of the world. More choices of communication channels across national and cultural borders mean more cross-cultural encounters take place not only in traditional face-to-face meetings, but via international telephone calls, faxes, e-mail, on-line database access and video conferencing. Exposure to foreign cultures via these media and through international travel has boosted interest in foreign language learning. To be a polyglot who can communicate in a multitude of languages, or even just to be bilingual, is a dream held by many, and one which is likely to grow even stronger for citizens of the global village. We can see evidence of this in the proliferation of Berlitz phrase books and audio/video language learning tapes, for example. The 'English Language Industry', ranging from language schools to language learning materials, is a multi-million dollar business in many non-English speaking countries, while the languages of Japan, China and Korea have gained enormous popularity in the West because of the economic influence of these countries. Motivated individuals as well as company sponsored employees are willing to invest time and money in language learning. Many educational institutions are forming affiliations with overseas counterparts so that student exchanges can be more readily facilitated, while foreign home-stay programmes for language acquisition purposes have become a consistently popular product in the tourism market.

But despite the best intentions, few aspiring linguists ever develop more than very basic foreign language skills due to lack of time and lack of long-term commitment. Very few reach the levels of proficiency necessary to conduct detailed technical or commercial discussion or produce adequate documents in a foreign language, even after many years of learning and despite the help of the latest technologies. The chronic shortage of human resources with adequate foreign language ability is not surprising and the vocations of translator and interpreter remain under-represented and in heavy demand in many parts of the world. The Japan Translation Federation estimates that the number of professional-class translators in Japan is less than 5000 and only about 30 of these are considered first class. The Director of the Federation, Makoto Sakamoto, laments the shortage of translators who are 'capable of producing sentences that would make consumers want to buy a product or service' (Sakamoto & Itagaki, 1993). Regrettably, this more or less describes the situation all over the world.

This chapter discusses the process of translation and the way the translation industry is adopting IT, in particular computerised translation systems (Machine Translation or MT) as tools to help fulfil the growing demand for its services.

Translators and Interpreters: What Do They Do?

The role of translators and interpreters as facilitators of interlingual communication demands an understanding of the concepts which underlie the written and spoken words of often diverse cultures. In other words, linguistic aptitude, itself difficult enough to find, is essential, but not sufficient, to make a good translator or interpreter. Linguistic traps abound, with potentially disastrous consequences for interpreters and translators. For example, the Japanese often try to avoid direct and confrontational language and may not clearly say yes or no, which can make their statements very hard to translate into languages such as English which use more straightforward expressions. One such phrase is known to have caused friction between former US President Nixon and the then Japanese Prime Minister Sato, who was accused of not keeping his promises after stating, through an interpreter, that he 'will take care of the issue'. The original Japanese expression 'zensho shimasu' was in fact intended to be a polite non-committal response, but this was not the meaning conveyed by the interpreter's rendition (Matsumoto & Mukai, 1976: 4). An Arabic expression which literally translates as 'this is a word of truth' is normally used to describe things which are untrue. It is not difficult to imagine the potential for misunderstanding which can arise unless the translator or the interpreter is thoroughly versed in such everyday usages. In reality, every language has elements of national idiosyncrasies buried in culture-bound expressions. Cross-cultural communicators have a daunting task to negotiate such hidden traps, as the failure to do so can cause grave misunderstanding.

In the world of literary translation, there is no shortage of examples to demonstrate the difficulties in transferring hidden messages contained in language. In some texts, conveying the cultural code attached to words can be crucial, and a drastic adjustment in the process of translation may be essential. One often-quoted example (Bekku, 1982: 86) occurred when a famous American translator of Japanese literature translated the Japanese words 'shiro [white] tabi [socks]' as 'white gloves' in English. What seems an obvious error was a deliberate strategy to convey the implied message. The original Japanese words carried the idea of formal attire, a concept that would have been completely lost by a literal translation, which would more likely have suggested casual sportswear! 'White gloves', on the other hand, recreated the implied image in the reader's culture.

The requirement for intimate cultural knowledge is generally less applicable to translators of technical material, but their task is no less difficult. Technical translation pursues the principle of literal rendition to a larger extent than literary translation does. Because the former tends to deal with more universal concepts rather than culture-specific ideas, it is less concerned with conveying connotative meaning across cultural barriers. But in order to translate specialised subject material, translators require sufficient subject knowledge to enable precise technical communication between experts in the field. Such technical knowledge is also essential for

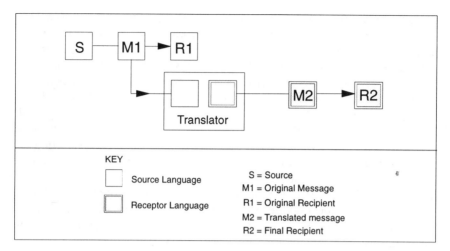

Figure 2.1 Role of translator (adapted from Nida & Taber, 1969)

conference interpreters at international meetings. Ideally all translators and conference interpreters should have their own area of subject expertise, but in reality they often have to cope with a wide range of topics which are outside their familiar territory. They are expected to speak and understand 'legalese', 'patentese' 'technologese', 'bureaucratese' and often deal with many more specialised domains at short notice.

Even a seemingly simple job such as translating a business card is by no means straightforward, and often requires an involved discussion particularly regarding the title of the card holder. The English word 'Manager' often needs explanation to pinpoint the exact position of the person in relation to the company hierarchy when translated into a number of other languages. Depending on the language and the context, it is not always possible to retain the same degree of vagueness used in the original title. In these cases, translators normally have to make a kind of approximation to transpose the person's position into the equivalent organisation in the target language culture. This sort of work clearly involves a far wider scope of knowledge in terms of social context than word-for-word translation, done by looking up dictionaries and constructing sentences according to grammatical rules.

Given these demands, it is difficult to cut costs, reduce production times and improve quality. And yet this is often the client's expectation. For example, to draw upon my own working experience in a translation company, clients who would readily accept the hourly charges of lawyers and accountants would balk at paying a fraction of those fees for translation work. One Wellington doctor absolutely refused to pay his NZ$100 account for the translation from Japanese into English of one page of a patient's detailed medical history necessary to assess the adequacy of a given treatment. The translation had involved consultation with a Japanese medical expert plus library-based research. The common problem reflected by this particular case was that the client did not appreciate that the translation involved two levels of expertise; linguistic skills on the one hand and subject knowledge on the other. Of course the ideal person to undertake such a translation would have been a bilingual Japanese medical doctor. But how many of them would have been available and could have been located in time? Professional translators who have had the opportunity to develop in-depth knowledge of a narrowly defined field are quite rare, often making it essential to consult subject specialists to produce accurate translation. Clients who fail to appreciate the value of such time-consuming endeavours consider that the charges are too high, while the service providers believe they are not being paid enough!

To understand translation and interpreting work as a communication process, it may be helpful to examine their role in terms of theoretical models of communication. Work done by Nida and Taber is particularly relevant, since they describe translation in terms of a communication process. Nida and Taber's model (Nida & Taber, 1969: 23), summarised in Figure 2.1, reinforces the qualitative aspects involved in the translation-mediated communication and points to the essential function performed by mediators.

This model illustrates the critical task assigned to the translator whose role is to ensure that the effect of a translated message (M2) on the recipient (R2) is equivalent to the effect the original message (M1) would have on a recipient (R1) who uses the original language. To appreciate the difficulty of achieving this, let me draw on the experiences of a British author, David Lodge (Workshop I Literary translation, 1994), whose novels are translated into many languages. Even to translate the title of his books sometimes poses a difficult challenge. For example, the title *Small World* is intended by Lodge to convey the connotation of the petty world of academia together with its proverbial meaning. To translate this into another language, ideally one would use an equivalent term conveying the same implications, but more often than not an exact equivalence does not exist in different languages. Such was the case for translation into German, so the author had to suggest the alternative title *Paper Chase* for the German edition as *Small World* just didn't have an exact equivalent. As this example illustrates, it is often extremely difficult to convey into another language the complete message attached to the original words, thus creating exactly the same impact on the readers of both languages. Lodge expresses the relationship between the reader and the translator in this way, 'If reading is an act led on by an endless unveiling process, the translator could be regarded as "reclothing" the text, reinserting everything which the translator had decoded.' (Lodge (1994: 62) So, the translator necessarily becomes a filter in decoding and re-encoding the message, thus forming a critical link. For this reason a simplistic word-to-word rendition is often not only meaningless but sometimes actively dangerous, causing serious damage to the message originally intended. The challenging task assigned to translators and interpreters is summarised in Tiffin's concept of translation as a 'paradigm shift':

> This is a function of a communication processing system [the human or computer translator] which in effect metaphysically shifts a message from one paradigmatic domain to another. This therefore means that the message becomes meaningful within another paradigmatic domain from that within and for which it was originally generated. This implies that the translation process is one of approximation. (Tiffin, 1990a)

The extent of 'paradigm shift' or 'approximation' which may take place during the process of translation or interpreting will depend on various factors such as the proximity of the languages and cultures involved and the type of communication. While the translation of contract papers will demand concentration on word-for-word accuracy, the translator of literary work will be more concerned with communication as a whole. An interpreter employed for a sensitive business negotiation needs to be alert to extra-linguistic cues such as nuance of phrase to convey the implied meaning, while at a scientific conference the focus will need to be on accurate rendition of technical terminology and denotative meaning. This is why translation and interpreting are highly knowledge intensive work and why the knowledge built up by an expert is not easily transferable to another individual, let alone to computers.

The Problems of Today's Language Services

So the tasks carried out by translators and interpreters involve much more than just the superficial understanding of words. But apart from the complex nature of the translation task itself, what other problems are faced by providers of language translation and interpreting services as a whole?

One important issue is that despite widespread recognition of the difficulty of mastering foreign languages, there is a general lack of appreciation by users of language services of what is involved in translators' and interpreters' work. This contributes to problems such as unrealistically short deadlines, inadequate instructions and insufficient information on a job's end use (which could significantly affect a translation). While the ability of an interpreter may become apparent relatively easily during an assignment, the quality of translation work is often not immediately obvious to the client, who, almost by definition, will lack the skills needed to judge it. This opens the way for pedestrian translators to undercut professional services. It is indeed possible for poor quality translation to go undetected for ever, as the clients may never associate their failure to attract foreign customers, for example, with their poorly translated publicity material.

The foremost problem confronting today's language services is this: while the IT revolution has swept modern offices, allowing the automation of a wide range of tasks, the interpreting and translation professions have remained largely reliant on human expertise. From a user perspective, however, these services need to be faster and cheaper to match the speed of information acquisition and dissemination made possible by IT. From this conflict arise these fundamental problems:

- **Limited production capacity**
  Skilled translators and interpreters are rare, their subject specialist knowledge is restricted and they can process only a limited quantity of work in a given time.
- **Inconsistent quality**
  The quality of a job is highly dependent on the skill of the individual translator or interpreter. A client may have paid the same rate, but the resulting jobs may vary in quality even within the same agency.
- **High cost**
  As highly knowledge-intensive and time-consuming work, translating and interpreting services are generally regarded as highly priced (at least from the user's perspective).
- **Unattainable deadlines**
  The time frames demanded for translation production are becoming shorter, as an effect of the growing speed and volume of information exchange.
- **A wide variety of languages and specialised subjects**
  The number of language pairs requested is growing, reflecting the widespread impact of the globalisation process. Also, because of rapidly advancing science and technology and their applications, a range of new and very specialised fields is appearing, requiring language experts to keep up with new developments.

In today's world, where technology so often helps overcome human limitations, much hope has been pinned on computers providing the answer to skill shortages and slow production in the language service business. In fact, the application of IT has increased productivity in translation offices significantly during the last decade despite the fact the core of the translating and interpreting process has remained mostly in the hands of human experts.

Table 2.1 shows typical IT applications already widespread within language services. They are divided according to three different domains of communications technologies: transmission, processing and storage, and also according to whether they form part of the Management, Production or Administration, which are considered to be core components of a typical language service provider. As indicated, the customer interface of the translation office has been transformed by the use of fax machines and data communication via modems in addition to the traditional means of physical delivery of text. The translating process is assisted by wordprocessors, electronic references and editing/revising tools. Virtual libraries available through computer networks such as the Internet provide valuable sources of information accessible from translators' desktops. CD-ROM based references save access charges of the on-line services while providing more up-to-date information than their paper counterparts. Desktop publishing (DTP) has helped add value to translation products by making translation output look more impressive with professional reproductions of visual elements such as graphs and tables. Imaging systems such as image processors which can be linked with the wordprocessing system are also in use to provide print-ready bromides. Finished jobs can be transmitted by fax, via modem or delivered on disk depending on the client's requirements.

Yet the gains in efficiency achieved through these applications of IT have not been sufficient to overcome the aforementioned bottleneck in interpreting and translation work which is causing a growing gap between demand and supply. It is easy to see, then, why the concept of MT has considerable attraction both for service providers and for their clients. To respond to the growing needs, language services have no choice but to find ways to increase the speed and cut the costs of translation production while maintaining quality. The time has come for translators to give some serious consideration to the potential applications of MT.

Is Machine Translation the Answer?

In recent years researchers have undoubtedly made progress with computer-based translation systems, known as Machine Translation (MT), and a number of MT systems are now commercially available. However,

Table 2.1 Summary of current application of Information Technology used by language services

Domain	Technology	Use
		MANAGEMENT
Trans-mission	Fax and modem	Requests for and delivery of quotations or other enquiries requiring confirmation in written form.
	Telephone (voice)	Negotiations and response to general enquiries.
Processing	—	(Entirely by human expertise)
Storage	Primary memory (hard disk)	Contains database on external translators and account information for individual jobs
		PRODUCTION
Trans-mission	Fax and modem	Enquiries to client about the text, sending/receiving jobs to/from external translators or typesetters, proofreading of texts for typesetters or by client prior to finalisation of translation.
	Telephone (voice)	Responses to general enquiries, enquiries to the client about the text, communications with external translators.
Processing	Word-processing	For text generation.
	Desktop publishing	For incorporating graphics production into texts and page layout in preparation for typesetting.
	Image processing	For computerised typesetting.
Storage	Primary memory (hard disk)	For storage of translated texts during and after production of the job and also for storage of retrieved information from on-line databases.

Table 2.1 (*continued*)

Domain	Technology	Use
	Secondary memory (floppy disk and CD-ROM)	For archiving of completed job, some input/output of texts from/to clients and translation jobs returned from external translators. CD-ROM databases (reference books) provide more up-to-date, flexible indexing system than their paper counterpart.

ADMINISTRATION

Domain	Technology	Use
Trans-mission	Fax	Confirmation of accounts and other enquiries.
	Telephone (voice)	Enquiries about accounts and other enquiries.
Processing	Job register processor	For registering incoming and outgoing jobs in a computer system.
	Invoice processor	For preparing invoices.
Storage	Primary memory (hard disk)	For storage of various accounts data.

these systems have so far failed to dominate the translation market by bridging the gap between demand and supply of language translation. It is now recognised by many language service providers and their customers that the technology in its present form cannot match the versatility of human translators.

Contrary to the computer engineers' initial predictions that 'if the dictionaries were large enough and the lexicography good enough, then the programs would be able to do quality translation' (Schank & Kass, 1988: 182), the natural languages we speak and write, with all their exceptions and ambiguities, their subtleties and idiosyncrasies, are far more complex than this statement suggests, and have proved to be beyond the capabilities of computer technology. Some of the issues which challenge human translators to their limits have been insurmountable for machines. The translation process often relies on extra-linguistic information which is extremely difficult to capture in computer terms. In other words, the correct interpretation of natural language often relies on human linguistic intuition. Human listeners and readers often add information from their own sources in order to make sense of the words they hear or read. For instance, in the sentence 'he cannot bear children' we automatically assume the meaning of 'bear' to be 'tolerate', because we know as a fact that men cannot give birth. But if the sentence was 'she cannot bear children', the only way to determine the correct interpretation of 'bear' would be from the context. The sentence 'I was watching a man with a telescope' is most likely to conjure up an image of the subject watching a man *through* a telescope, rather than watching a man carrying a telescope, because of our knowledge about the meaning of the word 'telescope'. On the other hand, if the sentence read 'I was watching a man with a gun' we would understand it as most likely to mean that the man was carrying a gun, as we know a gun is not a viewing device. This distinction, however, cannot be made purely on the basis of grammatical rules. Before a translator, human or machine, can even begin the task of converting such sentences into another language, it is usually necessary to resolve such ambiguities. Doing this involves access to an enormous amount of world knowledge or common sense, together with the inference capabilities required to apply the knowledge to a given context.

Such complexity in the translation process has not always been recognised. In fact a critical error made by some early MT researchers was to assume that the translation process could be reduced to word mapping and reconstituting sentences on the basis of rules of grammar (syntax). This led them to conclude that translation was an ideal candidate for computerisation. The very earliest research on MT seems to have originated in 1946 when Warren Weaver of the Rockefeller Foundation proposed the idea that 'if the code-deciphering techniques developed during the Second World War were used, computers would be able to recognise the fundamental aspects of all known languages' (Nagao, 1989: 19). In 1954, Georgetown University and IBM publicised the results of a joint experiment with a Russian–English MT system – the first instance of such a project anywhere in the world. The experiment attracted a great deal of public attention and although mixed results were reported, it raised hopes that the Tower of Babel was finally on the verge of crumbling. Political and security considerations in the cold-war atmosphere of the 1950s boosted MT research, with funding from the governments of both the USA and the USSR. The success of the Soviet Sputnik urged on the study in the USA of automatic translation between Russian and English in an effort to catch up with the Soviet space programme. In the USSR research on translation between Russian and English was under way, and China carried out pioneering research into translation between Chinese and Russian.

But despite the high expectations, technical difficulties became increasingly apparent to the MT community. The more research progressed, the clearer it became that complex linguistic problems were preventing the development of a usable system. In 1964 the US National Academy of Sciences set up the Automatic Language Processing Advisory Committee (ALPAC) to review the status and predict the future of MT research. The 'ALPAC Report' dismissed any possibility of successful automatic translation and regarded MT research as virtually fruitless. As a result, MT research throughout the world was curtailed. In the USA, where government support alone had reached US$20 million during the preceding 10 years (Nagao, 1989: 26), research funding was cut and a negative atmosphere prevailed in all MT-related areas.

While human translators and interpreters generally carry out extra-linguistic interpretation of sentences and phrases subconsciously, making computers do the equivalent is an extremely ambitious task. Cultural issues, such as the 'white gloves' example illustrated earlier, add a further challenge to MT. Any translation of literature or PR material, typically full of puns or cultural innuendoes, requires the decoding and encoding of imbedded qualitative values based on cultural or local knowledge. For example, a New Zealand brand of export timber proudly named as 'Red Stag' simply doesn't carry the same connotation in some Asian markets in their languages. MT certainly could not advise the client a suitable alternative, let alone explain the loss of original connotation if translated literally. Another example is the term 'back-to-back housing' (Lodge, 1994: 63), again used in a David Lodge novel. A literal translation into some languages would not carry the intended meaning of 'working class housing'. On the subject of 'play on words', consider translating a meat company's advertisement which finishes with 'Tenderly Yours'. Such an assignment provides an ample challenge even to a human translator who has to convey the double meaning expressed by 'tenderly', i.e. to find a word applicable to meat and combine it with the protocol for closing written correspondence. This sort of task certainly requires a paradigm shift from one culture to another and is quite out of reach of the current generation of MT.

One MT product aimed at the mass consumer market whose usefulness is severely restricted by the limitations of today's technology can be seen in the range of small hand-held calculator-like devices that have been available for some years. Aimed mainly at tourists, these tools typically provide automatic phrase book and pocket dictionary functionality by accepting individual words or phrases input by keypad entry and displaying the translated output on screen. Some are capable of producing voice output. The concept is appetising, but in reality these devices are not only severely limited in terms of sentence patterns and vocabulary, but also lack any ability to interact with the user. They do not have the flexibility to accommodate natural conversational patterns which often deviate from text-book examples and therefore are only useful to the same extent as phrase books or paper dictionaries. This is why these gadgets have largely remained toys rather than providing serious solutions to cross-cultural communication problems. To gain widespread popularity future products of this kind will have to support voice input and output, with a much wider range of sentence patterns and vocabulary.

What Can Machine Translation Do?

These apparently irreconcilable problems might suggest that MT has been a complete failure. But this is not the case at all. Enthusiasm for MT revived in the 1970s and started to bear fruit in the 1980s when commercial MT systems began to appear. The first personal computer-based translation software became available in 1983 (Vasconcellos, 1993a) and today a range of MT systems is in use. The turnaround is not only thanks to the great advances in computer hardware, but also because both researchers and users have come to a realistic understanding of both the practical limitations of MT and the complex nature of translation, and have started to apply MT only in selective areas where it can succeed.

In spite of the very real difficulties, already outlined, with handling the complexities and ambiguities of natural language, computers are without doubt superior to their human counterparts in some aspects of the translating process. In addition to the commonly cited 'they don't take coffee breaks' sort of advantages of machines over humans, machine memory, for example, is suited to accumulating vast quantities of information in an easily retrievable manner within short time frames. Computers can then transfer such information between themselves much more easily and systematically than can humans. Computers can be absolutely consistent in their use of terminology throughout a lengthy document while the human finds this hard. In other words, machine translation and human translation work on the basis of different skills. Professor Nagao (1992: 14), a world authority on MT research at Japan's Kyoto University, uses an analogy to describe the limits and potential of MT, pointing out that there is as fundamental a difference between the translation mechanisms used by humans and MT as there is between the way birds and aeroplanes fly. And yet both birds and aeroplanes can fly.

The practical application of computers to natural language translation therefore requires us to understand and make maximum use of their advantages while avoiding their weaknesses. This means the classification of translation jobs in terms of their suitability for MT. The translating process involves varying levels of text analysis depending on the type and nature of the material involved, from superficial and mechanical at one end of the scale, to deep and intuitive at the other. A technical manual, for example, is 'denotative' in nature, which is to say it contains largely universal concepts that do not vary from one culture to another and will not require culture-based analysis; even word-for-word translation may make sense. Translating a sentence such as *'The PC runs at 16 Mhz, the 9001 processors at 8 MHz and the circulation time round loop is 120 ms... '* would involve no 'paradigm shift' or approximation between source and target languages. On the other hand, texts in fiction writing are largely of a 'connotative' nature and the translation must convey approximate conno-tation. As a generalisation, MT can provide usable outputs where translation can be done in a superficial or mechanical manner, but accuracy and readability reduce as it is used for text requiring deeper analysis based on the context or cultural aspects. Translation of connotative text is now largely accepted as being beyond the capability of present MT systems, but denotative text can be handled by MT to an acceptable standard, particu-larly when it is within a defined subject area.

In the real world the wide variety of purposes for which translations are used means that MT output is perfectly acceptable in some circumstances. Either the subject matter or type of text suits the capabilities of MT (e.g. technical manuals) or because a certain amount of inaccuracy or stylistic inferiority is an acceptable trade-off against speed and price for the particular end-use of the translation (perhaps to locate quickly relevant parts of a large volume of documents for subsequent handling by a human translator). Even where MT cannot produce output which is acceptable to the end-user, it may perform a useful function by doing a 'first pass' on a text before it undergoes final processing by a human translator who can then complete the job in less time than would be possible without the computer.

Consider the following two cases of MT output. In a French film a sign reading *'Chien méchant'* is seen on a gate. The English subtitle *'Beware of the dog'* is certainly far preferable to the literal rendition of *'Nasty dog'* offered by MT. On the other hand, most consumers can accept, perhaps with a little

Table 2.2 Quality requirements according to end-uses

Low	High
Translation to a transitory stage (draft translation)	Translation to a final stage (edited translation)
Translation for internal use (information only)	Translation for public use (publication/presentation)
A general outline will suffice	Translation requiring utmost accuracy

amusement, the phrase *'Data-communication is getting essential in life today. Now, let's be getting on the way'* produced by MT in the manual for an Asian manufactured modem. The meaning is understood, and the unidiomatic language doesn't really matter. The quality of translation judged in absolute terms can sometimes be irrelevant in the real world of commercial translation particularly if that is the trade-off for lower charges and quicker turnaround. This is an important factor for service providers to take into consideration. 'Quality' clearly has a different significance in every translation job. For example, it depends on the end-use of the resulting translation, as suggested by Professor Nagao (1989: 52) in Table 2.2. This is an important factor in considering MT applications.

The Japan Electronic Industry Development Association (JEIDA) has been actively carrying out research in MT through its MT System Research Committee whose MT Market and Technology Study Subcommittee has developed a series of criteria both for potential users and MT system developers (JEIDA, *Methodology and Criteria on Machine Translation Evaluation*, 1992). Its user evaluation utilises a set of parameters which define MT 'friendly' and 'unfriendly' environments. Table 2.3 summarises these parameters, which include such factors as the growing use of information technology (IT) by clients of translation services, whether the subject matter is narrow or broad, and the budget allocated to the overall production of the translation. The importance of the IT factor arises because MT processes text in electronic format, therefore supplied input text in compatible electronic format can introduce efficiencies by streamlining the interface to an MT system. The issue of budget will determine whether MT is affordable at all. MT can involve high one-off costs for the purchase of the system, customising its dictionaries to suit the relevant subject domains and training staff in the machine's characteristics so that the input text can be

Table 2.3 JEIDA parameters to define MT suitability

	Parameters	MT friendly	MT unfriendly
1	Volume of translation	large	small
2	Difficulty of translation	easy	difficult
3	Quality required	no strict standard	a high standard
4	Languages involved	a specified pair	varied
5	Subject domain	limited	varied
6	Production time frame	short	long
7	IT environment in place (automation)	advanced	not advanced
8	Translation resources (in-house staff, sub-contractor, task division)	task clearly divided	not clearly divided
9	Budget allocated to translation	high initial investment; low ongoing	high ongoing
10	Text data extraction (separation of diagrams, photos, etc.)	not much organisation	a lot of organisation
11	Re-insertion of text data	not much work	a lot of work
12	MT installation conditions (budget for resource)	not limited	limited
13	Pre-editing (removing ambiguity, ensuring use of standardised language, etc.)	not much work	a lot of work
14	Post-editing (checking for 'obvious' errors, making text more colloquial, etc.)	not much work	a lot of work

efficiently pre-edited and output text can be post-edited in an optimum fashion. By comparison, employing human translators generally involves lower initial start-up costs but perhaps higher ongoing costs in the form of salaries.

Consideration of the 14 JEIDA parameters gives a good indication of whether MT could operate efficiently for the user. The most suitable environment for MT would have a regular demand for large volumes of text limited to well-defined subject areas always between the same language pairs. The text would not require much pre-editing work to separate non-text elements such as graphs and tables. The time frame for production would be short and a strict quality standard would not be required, thus reducing the necessity for extensive post-editing. Also, the text would be such that little time would have to be spent by human translators correcting ambiguities in the input text before MT took over, and the output would, similarly, require only minor 'post-correction' by human intervention before it went to the customer. The input text would preferably have been supplied in an electronic form. Under such circum-stances MT could outperform human translation. In other words, today's MT could work well in a carefully selected environment. As seen from the above assessment MT has not resolved all the problems faced by the translation industry, but it is going some way towards helping to meet real needs which could not otherwise be dealt with by human translators alone.

Machine Translation Success Stories and Emerging New Applications

In 1976, ending what would be called the 'dark ages' of MT research, the Commission of the European Communities (CEC) decided, following a long period of careful assessment, to implement a commercial MT system called Systran for translation between English and French. The motivation arose from the huge cost of manual translation (by over 2000 staff) of conference proceedings and other administration documents into the official languages of the European Community. The original MT system has been significantly upgraded since it was first commissioned and is reported to achieve a very high success rate for its translations.

Often quoted as the most successful and long-standing example of MT in operation anywhere in the world is the TAUM METEO system, which was implemented in Canada in 1978. Developed at Montreal University, it is used by the Canadian Weather Service for routine translation of English weather reports into French. With a vocabulary of some 1500 items, about half of which are place names (Nirenburg et al., 1992: 12), the system relies on the fact that sentences used in weather reports are generally short and employ standard phraseology (i.e. the input to the MT system is syntactically and semantically well-delineated). Within a specific field such as meteorology it is possible to predefine almost all possible grammatical structures used, thus reducing ambiguity to a minimum. Translated text is sent out directly to newspaper offices, broadcasting stations and other news outlets. With a success rate for unaided translations of about 95% (Nagao, 1989: 33) the TAUM METEO example has demonstrated that within the confines of the 'ideal' environment MT can attain highly usable results.

Two surveys give an interesting insight into MT applications in the 1990s. In June 1993 the International Association for Machine Translation (IAMT) surveyed (Lawson & Vasconcellos, 1993: 121–2) 75 MT users worldwide and received responses from 38, including 16 in USA, 11 in Europe and 11 in Japan: 82% of respondents had installed MT during the preceding five years; 17 different systems were in use; throughput ranged from 25,000 to 45,000,000 words per annum and the most commonly translated item was technical manuals. One user, a manufacturer of machinery for industrial fluids, stated: 'Translation would be barely feasible for this volume at this speed without it [MT]', while a commercial translation company commented (Vasconcellos, 1993b: 43): 'MT is indispensable for high-volume jobs'. The survey (Vasconcellos, 1993b: 35) also picked up an important trend in the considerable growth of the PC-based MT (PCMT) market, with one vendor quoted as having sold over 200,000 packages under US$100. The enormous popularity of such packages was also confirmed by a 1992 reader ballot taken by *WordPerfect Magazine* (Vasconcellos, 1993b: 35); when asked to list their favourite WordPerfect compatible software, no fewer than 7865 readers voted for the MT software category. Another survey, reported in the 1993 Report of JEIDA (*Research Findings on Utilisation of MT Systems*, 1993: 294–308), covered 11 MT users in Japan (who were not included in the IAMT survey). Users were classified into one of four categories:

(1) **Translation companies** – using MT selectively according to document type and in conjunction with extensive pre- and post-editing.

(2) **Corporate/government users** – including the Australian Embassy – cited a major reason for using MT as being to retain more control over the translation process and reduce the volume of translation being done by outside organisations.

(3) **Individual user** – translating a technical book for private use – observed that over 50% of sentences were translated adequately.

(4) **Computer network services** – using MT to provide on-line translation services to users with network access via modem and PC.

The JEIDA survey also showed that the 10 leading translation companies in Japan had each implemented some form of MT, and that among total translation operators 20% now used MT (up from 7.7% in 1991). One focal point of current MT research is to explore innovative applications such as the use of MT as a component in the information retrieval process during electronic database searches. Another novel application, developed by Japan's broadcasting organisation, Nippon Hoso Kyokai (NHK), is for television news subtitling. Their MT system comes with a subtitle production system bundled with integrated modules for videotape monitoring on-screen, manual superimpose-timing input, and preview of the completed program (Vasconcellos, 1993b: 43). This illustrates the possibility of MT applications within the multimedia environment.

Machine Translation and Telecommunications

Examples of symbiosis between MT and telecommunications are beginning to emerge, showing how telecommunications can help to supply language services in a new and more efficient manner. At the 4th MT Summit held in Kobe, Japan in 1993, keynote speaker Professor Nagao (1993) referred to the case of a Japanese company making use of international telecommunications networks to send English text overseas for pre-editing prior to MT processing or for post-editing of MT output in order to alleviate the difficulty of finding English native editors in Japan. Despite the telecommunications charges involved, the total cost of MT-based translation was less than having the work done entirely manually. This illustrates an emerging use of telecommunications to complement the shortage of human resources in a given location.

Another example is the effective time-hiring of MT systems to users of computer network services cited earlier in the JEIDA survey. These on-line translation services take advantage of increasingly popular computer networks by providing customers with access to MT directly via personal computer terminals. They target individual users at their desktops by offering convenience, speed and economy as advantages over conventional human-based translation services. Among such services currently running in Japan are Atlas Machine Translation and IBS Machine Translation, whose users are aware of the inferior output quality compared with human-based translation, and the fact that this is a clear trade-off against cost and speed. Table 2.4 summarises the key attributes of these Japanese MT services.

Atlas do not carry out any pre-editing of the input and accordingly some texts are beyond the capabilities of the computer and returned as

Table 2.4 Japanese computer network-based MT services (contents updated as of March 1995 based on the original information by *Nikkei
Datapuro/OA Sokuho*, 1990)

Attributes	Atlas Machine Translation	IBS Machine Translation
Provided by	FUJITSU Learning Media	IBS
Computer networks	NIFTY-Serve	PC-VAN
Service offered since	October 1990	December 1992
Languages handled	Japanese↔English	Japanese↔English
MT system used	Atlas	Pivot/JE, Pivot/EJ
Turnaround time	about 15 minutes/ A4 page	within 24 hours
Charges	J→E: 1 yen per English word E→J: 2 yen per Japanese word	J→E: 3000 yen up to 360 words; then 1500 yen/page E→J: 3000 yen up to 720 Japanese letters; then 1200 yen/page

'translation unsuccessful'. On-line advice is available to users on how to
tailor input text to make it more suitable for machine processing. In a sense
the client is made to do part of the work which would normally have to be
done by a translation company. IBS has human translators pre-edit any
input text which is rejected by initial MT processing. They can therefore
guarantee the output to be at least intelligible. The users of these services
are mainly Japanese business people needing to scan English documents
quickly to gain a rough idea of their content.

The free translation service provided by the Nishinomiya City (*JEIDA
Research Findings on Utilisation of MT Systems*, 1993), near Osaka in Japan is
another example. Nishinomiya City Council introduced MT-based trans-
lation services in April 1991 as a network community service – part of a
'New Media Model' plan by Japan's Ministry of International Trade and
Industry. The translation service has succeeded in its major objective of

promoting network usage. In August 1992 alone 126 users requested the translation services 500 times, and total subscribers of the network itself have now exceeded 4000, thanks to the free translation service by MT capturing a great deal of public attention. Nishinomiya City has classified users of its translation service into four main types:

(1) Urgent translation material for information purposes only.
(2) Rough translation required for assessing the value of having a subsequent full translation made by human translators.
(3) Personal material requiring a cheap and rough translation.
(4) Translation of information obtained on-line via the network.

These equate to the typical MT uses as reviewed in this chapter. While this service itself may not seriously threaten commercial translation service providers, the development can be seen as significant as one of the first 'public' MT systems.

In Europe 'Express-Translation' (Scheresse, 1992: 114–15) is a commercial service provided by Systran MT which is based on a host computer in France and is accessible by dial-up link from PCs throughout Europe. The received text is first automatically pre-edited (spell-checked, sentence structure modified and converted into ASCII file) and then translated by the Systran MT system at approximately one minute per page. During the translation process the general dictionary is reviewed first and then, depending on the text, up to 20 specialised technical dictionaries in such areas as computing, mechanical engineering, electronics, etc. can be accessed. Once the translation is complete, the ASCII text is reconverted by the system's format-text software which reinserts the original format code. Finally, post-editing takes place to check terminology and syntax before the finished product is returned electronically to the customer.

In August 1994 the giant US-based information service provider CompuServe, with 2.5 million subscribers worldwide, introduced English, French and German MT-based on-line near real-time translation services in its MacCIM Help Forum (see also Chapter 4). The MacCIM Forum is a part of CompuServe's basic services, and offers support and assistance to users of the CompuServe Information Manager for the Macintosh computer. For software support forums the immediacy of the response is considered crucial, thus making a quick MT service invaluable to users who wish to work in French or German. Messages requiring translation services are collected hourly and MT translates them at a rate of up to 1800 words per minute. French- or German-speaking users can specify their preferred language in their user profile and they are automatically routed to the version of the forum in the language of their choice.

Another new MT-based service is Globalink's 'Internet Message Translation System (MTS)'. This service allows registered users to have e-mail text and files automatically translated by MT between English, French, German and Spanish. Once the user registers with MTS, text can be sent to Globalink's e-mail address and the translated text will be returned to the user's e-mail address or redirected to another Internet address. The service takes a truly automated approach from the initial registration, to job reception, customer enquiries, job dispatch and billing.

As these examples demonstrate, when linked with telecommunications and used selectively, MT, despite its shortcomings, becomes a valuable multilingual IT tool.

Machine Translation in the Future

Perhaps within a decade, MT will appear in your life in several ways – translating telephones, multilingual E-mail, and machines that scan and translate letters and articles written in foreign languages. You may be buying toys over the phone from a sales agent in Japan with the telephone doing the translating. And when you travel to a foreign country, you'll be able to get the same bargain rates that the natives do with your trusty PET (Portable Electronic Translator). (Hovy, 1993)

Given the complexity involved in the translation and interpreting processes and also the limitations of current technology, it may be hard to envisage this optimistic scenario painted in 1993 by *Byte* magazine ever becoming reality. And yet, if we reflect on just how far the wider field of IT has advanced in the past 10 years, the prospects for the next ten also seem considerable. There is no doubt that the issue of how to carry meaning across cultural barriers will continue to be the major challenge in the search for better quality MT, and to this end the advances now taking place in such computing fields as fuzzy logic, parallel processing, neural networks, and knowledge-based systems using artificial intelligence (AI) techniques may make a positive contribution. A recent trend in MT research into example-based and statistical-based systems may also bring considerable improvements on some of the problems encountered by today's MT. Irrespective of which methods may bring the breakthrough, it is clear that users are recognising the potential benefits of MT and are beginning to make use of the technology within restricted environments. Growth in usage and experience may well lead to innovative applications and will further boost R&D efforts to advance the technology.

One specific application of MT that has exciting possibilities for the future is automatic translation of the spoken word. Research projects with this objective are under way in several parts of the world, aiming to integrate the technologies of speech recognition, MT and speech synthesis. While the last component is quite well developed (we often encounter computer-generated voices nowadays) the other two elements and the smooth integration of one with the other are proving to be major challenges. Speech recognition involves the process of mapping the acoustic wave forms corresponding to spoken language into strings of words. The difficulty involved is obvious when one considers how each of us has a different voice with its own characteristics of frequency, amplitude, phase and speed of utterance. Although voice-activated computers are in use today, the technology has yet to reach the stage where it can accept a wide vocabulary spoken at a natural rate and intonation and convert it with consistent accuracy into a form suitable for input into an MT system. The requirements of MT in speech-to-speech translation are essentially the same as in text-to-text translation, except that greater speed and accuracy are needed when used for real-time conversations, as there is no opportunity for editing by human translators before the output text from MT is sent to the voice generation device.

As with automatic translation of text, MT for the spoken word has interesting possibilities when linked to telecommunications system, and today research in this field is under way in the labs of many leading telcos. In his 1986 book *Computers and Communications* (Kobayashi, 1986) Dr Kobayashi, then Chairman of the Japanese multinational electronics and telecommunications company NEC, described his long-standing vision of the computer-based interpreting telephone as a way to break through language barriers. BT's research laboratories first announced (Stentiford & Steer, 1988) its prototype interpreting telephony system in Geneva in October 1987 to interpret automatically between English, French, German and Spanish. The system is designed to handle most frequently used phrases in a given field (e.g. hotel reservation). After the speech recognition process, the system matches the utterance with the closest phrase in its memory based on keywords from the user's speech. This reduces recognition errors greatly. The research proved that if the topic of dialogue is limited, the core information contained in a message is equally limited and therefore can be classified and stored against keywords.

The extent of progress with automatic speech translation was demonstrated in January 1993 at Japan's leading research institute in the field, the Interpreting Telephony Research Laboratories of ATR (Advanced Telecommunications Research Institute International) in Kyoto. An experiment in 'Interpreting Telephony' linked participants in Japan (ATR), the USA (Carnegie Mellon University) and Germany (Siemens/Karlsruhe Univer-

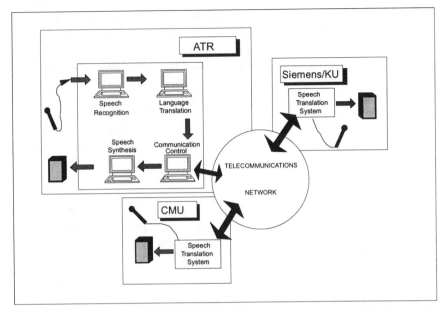

Figure 2.2 ATR interpreting telephony joint experiment (Morimoto & Kurematsu, 1993: 91)

sity), and was able to demonstrate real-time computer-based interpreting of spoken Japanese, English, and German. The experiment used three equivalent systems, each developed by the relevant research institute, and these were arranged as shown in Figure 2.2.

A speech recognition system at each participating location analysed the local speaker's words and converted them to text which was translated into the text of the recipient's language by MT. The translated text was transmitted via international telecommunications links to the recipient's location, where speech synthesis equipment converted it into spoken output. It was obvious to the audience that the speakers had to articulate unusually clearly and speak slowly, and that there was a significant time lag before the message was finally output in the recipient's language. Furthermore, matching of attributes of the output voice such as age, sex and emotion to those of the input had not been addressed. Despite these weaknesses, conversation did take place and the experiment signalled the beginning of a new era of automatic interpreting.

In Europe the 'SUNDIAL' (Speech UNderstanding and DIALogue) project (Fraser, 1993) supported by the Commission of the European Communities as part of the ESPRIT project, aims to design an interpreting telephony system for assisting computer database access in several languages. It will provide a publicly accessible system for voice-based interaction with computer systems giving flight information and reservation dialogues in English and French, and train timetable enquiries in German and Italian. This is yet another example of MT being designed to serve a specific situation as opposed to general dialogue. As the technology improves, general-purpose automatic interpreting telephony will be targeted. This project has already identified a number of useful aspects of human-to-machine interaction. For example, when users believed they were talking to a computer system, their language was constrained significantly, as compared with dialogue with another human. Interestingly, a similar level of constraint was demonstrated when people speak with a foreigner (Fraser, 1993: 167). Also, it was confirmed that as long as the domain of the dialogue is restricted, speech recognition technology, the essential front-end to any automatic interpreting, has reached a workable level of development.

Another practical example of a restricted domain system is the telecommunications link developed for use on the high-speed trains running through the Channel Tunnel between London and Paris. Drivers and controllers will use a bilingual computerised communications system consisting of both visual and audio messages in French and English based on 'Rail-speak' (Bell, 1992), a specialised language used in driver-signaller interactions.

And in Germany the Verbmobil project (Wahlster, 1993) funded by the Ministry for Research and Technology (BMFT) and an industrial consortium aims at developing a portable translation device for face-to-face dialogues in English, German and Japanese for use in a small room setting with speakers who don't share the same language but have some knowledge of English. This project is practical in its goal setting in that it aims to help fill in the gaps in speakers' knowledge of English rather than provide a complete automatic interpreting service. This type of 'electronic assistance' will appeal to certain users who only need the partial assistance of interpreters and in fact it may provide an advantage by forcing the speakers to try harder to understand each other, and to make better use of non-verbal cues, compared with when they have the full use of human interpreters.

Perhaps there will come a time – when is impossible to estimate – that the ultimate MT system will arrive. It will be able to deal with any type of text, both connotative and denotative, in either written or spoken form, and will carry out contextual and situational analyses equivalent to the interlingual communication process performed by human translators and interpreters whose understanding goes beyond the superficial meanings of words. As a type of AI, such a system will access a gigantic database of world knowledge and will have instant inference capability thanks to exponential advancements in computing power. It will accept your spoken words in your own language, and automatically translate them into a specified language in either written or spoken form. It will adjust the style and format to suit your relationship with the recipient and the nature and context of your message. It may even compose your message on the basis of key information you supply, and tailor it to suit the situation specified. In order to maximise its powerful capabilities such a system could be an integral part of a communications system which may have a significant and far reaching impact upon cross-cultural communication.

It is interesting to speculate upon the implications, should MT become ubiquitous and transparent in our communication channels. Will it, for example, mean an end to the need to learn foreign languages? Would the number of international telephone calls skyrocket, realising otherwise depressed demand due to language barriers? Discussion of some of the implications is left for Chapter 5.

I leave the last word on the subject of future MT to the imagination of Douglas Adams. In *The Hitch Hiker's Guide to the Galaxy* he describes the ultimate portable automatic translation machine.

> The Babel fish... feeds on brainwave energy received not from its own carrier but from those around it. It absorbs all unconscious mental frequencies from this brain wave energy to nourish itself with. It then excretes into the mind of its carrier a telepathic matrix formed by combining the conscious thought frequencies with nerve signals picked up from the speech centres of the brain which has supplied them. The practical upshot of all this is that if you stick a Babel fish in your ear you can instantly understand anything said to you in any form of language. The speech patterns you actually hear decode the brain wave matrix which has been fed into your mind by your Babel fish. (Adams, 1979: 49–50)

3 Global Network of Communications

In a world in which hundreds of millions of computers, servants to their users, easily plug into a global information infrastructure, business mail would routinely reach its destination in five seconds instead of five days, dramatically altering the substance of business communications. A company's designers and marketers would actively collaborate on a product, even when located a continent apart and unable to meet at the same time. Consumers would broadcast their needs to suppliers, creating a kind of reverse advertising. Many goods would be ordered and paid for electronically. And from a comfortable position in your easy chair, you could enjoy a drive through your next vacation spot, a trip through the Louvre or a high-definition movie rented electronically, chosen from the millions available.

Scientific American (Dertouzos, 1991)

The communications environment described above may sound impossibly futuristic to some; but to others, who have savoured the latest technologies, this scenario is already a reality. Behind this sophisticated communications infrastructure lie advanced computer-driven communications networks. *The Economist*'s (7 January, 1994) view of today's 'seven wonders of the world' included the world's telephone network, which the magazine estimates now links 580 million subscribers, in all corners of the world, who in 1992 spent over 40 billion minutes on the phone making international calls. And in December 1993 the business magazine *Fortune* described in its cover story (Stewart, 1993) how the world is undergoing four business revolutions. One revolution is the widespread application of computers; another is the use of telecommunications to link those computers to form an information economy. *Fortune* estimates that two out of every five computers in the USA are today interlinked via some form of telecommunications network (Stewart, 1993: 5). To take advantage of these networks *Time*, on 12 September, 1993 became the first international news magazine to enter the interactive-network age (13 September, 1993) when it was made available via the electronic network America Online, whose 350,000 users were able to access the text of each issue electronically every Sunday afternoon, US time. By January 1994 some 60,000 subscribers were reading *Time* electronically in this way each week, and subscription to America Online had grown to 500,000 (*Time*, 10 January, 1994).

Central to this picture of exponential growth of the communications network is the Internet – a gigantic network of networks which started life in the late 1960s in the USA as Arpanet, a non-commercial research-oriented network. Today the Internet's growth rate of a million new users every month heralds the dawn of the network-based society. Internet is discussed in more detail at the end of the chapter. As the Internet developments alone show, significant changes are taking place in our communications environment.

This chapter discusses key trends in telecommunications and explores their relationships with language services mainly from the perspective that the new telecommunications technologies are creating new demand for new cross-cultural communication services. The subjects are approached largely from a service viewpoint but technical aspects are touched upon where relevant. The evolution of 'Plain Old Telephone Service' (POTS) into today's multi-feature systems which include the narrowband Integrated Services Digital Network (N-ISDN) and the Intelligent Network (IN) is examined, together with anticipated developments in broadband ISDN (B-ISDN), International Value-Added Network Service (IVANS) and Universal Personal Telecommunications (UPT). And finally the implications of the Internet in relation to language services are examined.

The Changing Foundations of Telecommunications Services

Before discussing the service angle of telecommunications technology development, it may be useful to appreciate something of the key technological ingredients from which the services are built. George Gilder, Senior Fellow of the Hudson Institute, writing in the *Harvard Business Review*, illustrated the bases of future telecommunications in this simple but clear way:

> Business built on sand and glass and waves. Sand in the form of a silicon sliver the size of a thumbnail, inscribed with a logical pattern as complex as a street map of the United States, switching its traffic in trillionths of seconds. Glass in threads as thin as a human hair, as long as Long Island, fed by laser diodes as small as a grain of salt and as bright as the sun. All suffused with electro-magnetic waves,

communications power as available as the air and as fast as light. (Gilder, 1991)

How long before this graphic description becomes reality? In fact it is already here. For example, virtually all telephone calls in New Zealand today are processed by digital telephone exchanges driven by complex programs on computer chips; i.e. by digital computers. And increasingly these calls travel across the country and beyond as digital signals carried in lightweight and durable optical fibres which are replacing copper wires, bringing more reliability and capacity. The concept of integrating computers and communications was championed as early as 1977 by Dr Kobayashi (1989) of Japan's NEC Corporation at Intercom 77 when he coined the term 'C&C'. Today the concept is reality and the C&C marriage is starting to produce 'intelligent' telecommunications systems with their own processing capability rather than mere conduits.

Further enhancement of telecommunications services will depend largely on the perfecting the marriage between the different environments of telecommunications and computing. This, according to Gilder, will close the gap between the 'microcosm' of the computer and the 'telecosm' of telecommunications. Telecosm is a term coined by Gilder (1991) to mean 'a domain of reality governed by the action of electromagnetic waves and in which all distances collapse because communication is at the speed of light'. For while the gap is clearly closing at the technology level, barriers still exist at the service level. As an example, ideally, after wordprocessing a document on your PC you could instantly send the text anywhere you like with no more difficulty than making a telephone call. Currently, this is often not the case, as the mere use of a modem to connect your computer to the telephone line is by no means straightforward, and the problems of incompatibility between computer software are notorious. A 1992 OECD (1992: 22) study observed that: 'Until recently, institutional barriers have kept apart the computing and communications departments in all but the most forward-looking companies.... However, alliances and mergers between firms in the two sectors continue as the recently-announced tie-ups between AT&T and NCR, Fujitsu and ICL demonstrate.' These corporate marriages may ultimately lead to the perfecting of the C&C concept, bringing improved transparency to global communications.

Voice-based Services

Over the past few decades, technological advances have transformed the telephone from a mere voice channel, which enabled simultaneous one-to-one communications, into a sophisticated multi-processor

Table 3.1 Terminal-based services

Terminal	Description	Applications
Jackpoint access	Plug-in connection points for telephone equipment.	Makes telephone equipment more of a portable appliance which can be moved from room to room as required, reducing the effort required to make or answer a phone call.
Cordless phone	Wireless, battery powered portable telephone which operates within about 50 metres of a base station connected to a conventional telephone jackpoint.	Makes telephone equipment totally portable within the boundaries of a typical residential property, further reducing the effort required to make or answer a phone call.
Cellular phone	See Table 3.2 – requires both terminal and network equipment.	
Loudspeaking phone	Provides hands-free telephone operation by amplifying remote caller's voice to normal conversation volume.	Frees user to do other things while talking on the phone; also enables several people in a room to participate in a phone call.
Answer-phone	Automatically answers incoming calls by playing a prerecorded message, then enables a caller to record a message in response.	Avoids lost calls when a user is unable to answer the phone. Can also be used as a screening device to avoid unwanted calls.
Speed dialling	Telephone numbers can be stored and automatically dialled by pressing a single button.	Simplifies the dialling of commonly called numbers or the most recently dialled number.

Table 3.2 Network-based services

Name of service	Description	Applications
Call waiting	Indicates the arrival of an incoming call to a party already talking on the phone, and enables the call to be answered. The other party can be put on hold temporarily, or released.	Avoids giving busy tone to callers who then subsequently need to call back. Improves the chances of making successful calls.
Call forwarding	Directs incoming calls towards any previously programmed number, anywhere in the world, according to specified conditions (e.g. always, or only when the dialled number is busy, or when the dialled number is not answered after a certain number of rings).	Avoids the loss of incoming calls when the called party is busy, unable or unwilling to take the phone. Allows calls to 'follow' the called party to other locations without the need to advise new numbers to callers.
Conference call	Allows many more than the conventional two parties to communicate simultaneously.	Enables virtual meetings to be held between several people without the need to travel to a single location.
Voice mail	Provides subscribers with a voice 'mailbox' into which callers can deposit spoken messages that can be retrieved by the subscriber when convenient. Also allows messages to be delivered to specified mailboxes and telephone numbers at a specified time and date.	Can be used rather like an answer-phone to store incoming calls in a central computer for subsequent retrieval by the recipient. Enables 'one-way' telephone contact between communicators when normal conversation is not convenient, due to time zone differences, for example.

Table 3.2 (*continued*)

Name of service	Description	Applications
Completion of calls to busy subscribers	Automatically reattempts a call that reaches a busy number when that number becomes free.	Avoids the need to redial busy numbers.
Automatic recall	Automatically calls the number of the last incoming caller.	Allows a call to be returned without the need to determine and dial the number.
Speed dialling	See Table 3.1 – can also be provided as a network based service.	
Cellular mobile telephone service	Wireless, portable telephone equipment which can operate anywhere within the boundaries of the cellular network, which may cover a city, an entire country, or even cross national borders.	Makes telephone equipment totally portable, further reducing the effort required to make or answer a phone call and giving the user truly ubiquitous communications capability.

communications device. What this has meant to the user is better quality and low cost availability of a wide range of services, increasing the overall effect and efficiency of communication. To appreciate the breadth of these advances at a glance, refer to the above tables, which summarise some of the common and popular enhancements to voice-based telephone services which have been progressively introduced throughout much of the world in recent years.

Table 3.1 contains features such as plug-in telephones, cordless phones and answer-phone devices, all of which derive from enhancements entirely within telephone instruments or terminals, and are generally quite 'visible' to users. The Table 3.2 examples, on the other hand, use developments within the network of interlinked computer-driven telephone exchanges which serve to switch the calls between users, and as such are sometimes

Table 3.3 Telephone charging arrangements

Option	Description	Applications
Telephone company Calling Card	By dialling a special access code, plus card number and PIN number, all charges for the call are debited to an account associated with the card, rather than to the telephone making the call.	When making chargeable calls from a phone other than your own, including from a public payphone when you don't have cash available.
0800/ Freephone	Calls to such numbers are automatically charged to the called party rather than the calling party.	An important business tool used to encourage customers by making calls free of charge to callers.
0900	The cost of Information services accessed via numbers commencing 0900 are automatically included on the caller's telephone bill.	A growing variety of services are provided this way, ranging from weather forecasts to pornographic stories. Including the charge for the information in the telephone bill avoids the need for the information provider to establish separate billing arrangements with callers.
(Manual) Collect	By placing the call through an operator, and with the called party's agreement, the charges are debited to the called party rather than the calling party.	When making chargeable calls from a phone other than your own, including from a public payphone when you don't have cash available.
Transfer Charge	By placing the call through an operator, the charges are debited to a nominated third party rather than the calling party.	When making chargeable calls from a phone other than your own, including from a public payphone when you don't have cash available.

Table 3.3 (*continued*)

Option	Description	Applications
Price Required	By subscription (for all calls) or by dialling a special access code (for casual calls) an operator will phone back and advise the cost of each chargeable call as soon as it is completed.	Used to determine how much to reimburse a phone owner when making chargeable calls from his phone.
Extension Identification	An operator intercept based service which enables a code number (supplied by the caller) to appear on the account, associated with the charge made for the call.	When several parties use a phone line and share the charges according to their usage, or where the user wishes to associate calls with different jobs or clients.

'hidden' from users. Some services in this category, such as call forwarding and call waiting, can be accessed from any standard telephone instrument, while others, like cellular telephones, also need special terminal equipment in order to function.

Of course many of these services can be used in combination with one another to create what are effectively new services. For example, by subscribing to call forwarding from your standard (fixed) telephone line to your cellular mobile phone you will have true portability of communications which is transparent to callers (who can always contact you by dialling your standard telephone number). In addition, you can use voice mail if you are away from both telephones.

As well as the services themselves, a wide range of special charging options is available to make payment for calls more convenient. Table 3.3 summarises different arrangements for charging telephone calls based on the services currently available from Telecom New Zealand, which are typical of services offered by telephone companies all over the world.

As the examples in the three preceding tables illustrate, all these features aim to maximise the convenience of telephone services by minimising the impact of the natural barriers to communication, i.e. distance, time and cost. They aim to extend our connectivity by ensuring that more telephone calls complete successfully. Considered in combination with the ever-growing density of telephone connections in the world and the rising quantity and quality of international telephone links, it is evident that these services all play a part in making multi-cultural and multilingual telephone contacts increasingly likely to take place. In that sense, they help stimulate demand for language translation needs. Certain services are especially likely to stimulate demand for language assistance.

One type of international call that is set to grow in popularity in the near future is the automatic reverse charge or 'freephone' call, commonly accessed by dialling a number with initial digits that include '800' (e.g. Telecom New Zealand's freephone calls commence with 0800). This type of call has surged in popularity over recent years as more and more businesses have adopted '800' numbers to encourage potential customers to contact them. According to the president of AT&T Network Systems International, 800 number calls make up half the total calls placed on the AT&T network today (*CommunicationsWeek International*, 20 March, 1995). Customers now expect to be able to call a business free of charge, and residential 800 service is becoming popular, for example, among families whose children are studying away from home. And that expectation is extending to include companies doing business beyond their national boundaries. Currently a company in one country can have a freephone number which can be dialled in other countries, but generally different numbers have to be used in each country. In January 1994 the International Telecommunications Union (ITU) announced (Hayes, 1994) its intention of establishing a unified world allocation for freephone numbering, to enable organisations to advertise a single number at which they can be contacted from anywhere in the world, free of charge to the caller. This work led to the announcement in February 1995 that the ITU had appointed '+800' to be the prefix for international freephone services to commence 1996 (*Communications Week International*, 6 March, 1995). Initiatives such as this reflect the growing globalisation of businesses and can only lead to increased international telephone traffic and more demand for communication across language barriers. Companies that intend boosting direct contact by telephone with their customers in foreign countries must take account of this demand by ensuring that callers to their advertised number from anywhere in the world do not require special language skills in order to do business. This will often necessitate having access to language interpreters.

Conference calls, which enable three or more parties to listen to and participate in a conversation from their standard telephones, offer opportunities to hold 'virtual' international conferences without leaving the office.

Voice mail, a relatively recent innovation, currently tends to be used mainly to store incoming telephone messages when the called party is unable to take calls, in much the same way as an answer-phone device. However, voice mail's capabilities go far beyond that, and a growth in its use is predicted to lead to more deliberate application of asynchronous mode voice communications (as opposed to synchronous mode where the communicating parties are connected simultaneously), as a means of making time spent on the telephone, especially for business purposes, more efficient and effective. In other words, rather than playing 'telephone tag', and just leaving 'please call me back' messages, people will start to accept that two-way conversations are not always necessary, and will use voice mail to conduct business with one another. In this way, messages can be sent at the convenience of the sender and received at the convenience of the recipient. An indirect advantage of this use of voice mail is its ability to overcome problems of time zone differences between countries for international telecommunication. Frequent users of international telecommunications are well aware that between some countries 'there is essentially no telephone window during regular working hours on either end... this is telephone tag with a vengeance' (Quarterman, 1993: 51). Time differences play a significant part in international telecommunications and this is why the asynchronous communications can be used to considerable advantage.

Some of these existing voice services can also be used to provide suppliers of language services with means of meeting this new demand. Conference calls, for example, can be the medium to link an interpreter into a conversation between parties who don't share a common language. Voice mail can do the same, only in asynchronous mode, and can therefore help overcome the problem of time zone differences as well. The next chapter studies actual applications of these services and other ways in which telecommunications can be used to beat the language barrier.

Text-based Services

While telephones undoubtedly dominate the telecommunication world today by their sheer numbers, the very first telecommunications systems carried information in 'written' rather than spoken form across the world, as telegraph messages. Nowadays, the original telegraph systems are dead, but new forms of sending text are rapidly gaining popularity, and have important implications for the language translation business.

Telefax

The most popular medium of text transmission today must be 'fax', or more formally telefax. The transparency of fax communications in transmitting and receiving written text of virtually any kind over any distance is hard to beat. Since the International Telegraph and Telephone Consultative Committee (CCITT) of the International Telecommunications Union (ITU) established the international 'Group 3' (G3) telefax machine standards in 1980 (*British Telecom World*, 1989) the connection of fax machines to telephone lines in business premises all over the world has grown steadily. Documents are being exchanged easily, cheaply and almost instantaneously, regardless of physical distance, while mail, courier and personal delivery are being superseded in terms of timeliness and cost. Today, even the smallest business advertises a fax number, and the constantly falling prices of fax machines means there are increasing numbers of residential fax users too. Telefax is an asynchronous form of communication, giving users the freedom to respond at their own convenience, similar to the situation with voice-mail – a particular advantage when communicating across time zones.

An interesting background to this technology from a translator's viewpoint is that its widespread use coincided with the needs of one nation in particular, Japan, with its pictogram-based alphabet comprising thousands of characters (Mahon, 1990: 48). Early methods of electronic transmission of Japanese language by telegraph had been time-consuming, laborious and prone to errors, and the complexity of the text initially hindered the adoption of Japanese language wordprocessing. The arrival of telefax enabled hand-written Japanese text to be easily and accurately transmitted, leading to an enormous increase in the rate of information exchange among Japanese businesses. Japan soon led the world in the number of fax machines per capita.

In relation to language services telefax now plays a significant role in the customer interface to translation companies in many parts of the world, as translation is a business based mainly on written communication. Today fax is probably the most common way a translation office receives work from external clients. However, despite its many advantages, current telefax technology does have a number of drawbacks in relation to translation work, especially as a medium for delivering the final product. One problem is that the resolution of the output text is often not sufficient to reproduce accurately very small or intricate characters, and this is a particular problem for some Asian languages. While a faxed page of typewritten Chinese, for example, is generally readable, it is seldom of sufficient quality to be printed directly in a formal document. So unless intended solely for in-house use, almost all Japanese and Chinese translations must either be sent to clients by some other method (ranging from paper copy sent by courier or mail to modem transmission including e-mail) or, if fax is used, must be subsequently re-typed and re-printed by the client.

Another drawback of fax is that electronic processing of a received fax message is no simple matter since the text is in the form of an image, usually on a sheet of paper. Even when the fax system is integrated into a computer (using fax modems and fax software), messages are still received in image format, which has no 'meaning' to the computer. In order to be recognised by a computer as text, the image first has to be scanned by optical character recognition (OCR) software – a process which often introduces errors, especially in the case of small or intricate characters. The ability to process received text is becoming increasingly important in the translation industry; often several translators in separate locations have to work on one job, and translators' clients often need to carry out further processing of translation output, for example following post-translation editing by subject specialists, or to adjust text layout prior to printing by desktop publishing (DTP) systems.

Other drawbacks of current telefax technology are the transmission speed of the standard G3 machines (typically 30 seconds per A4 page) makes sending of high volume documents a slow and sometimes expensive process; lack of confidentiality (fax machines are often located in relatively public places in an office); and the ever present danger of 'wrong number' errors resulting in texts being sent to unintended parties without the sender being aware. Some of these disadvantages of current fax transmission based on the G3 standards will be overcome or at least reduced in future when fax machines based on the latest 'Group 4' (G4) technical standards become popular. G4 fax machines are discussed later in this chapter under ISDN.

Data communications

Whereas fax is essentially a paper-to-paper form of communication, text can also be conveyed across long distances in the form of electronic data sent between two computers. This can be achieved in a variety of ways, including physically delivering a floppy disk containing the data in the form of a computer file, or by using telecommunications solutions such as linking the computers directly via modems and dial-up telephone connection or by a variation on this known as e-mail which essentially uses one or more intermediate computers to store the file until it is convenient for the intended recipient's computer to receive it. Modems and associated communications software designed to use standard telephone connections to link computers are commonplace today and it is possible to dial into a variety of networks that assist in the computer communication process. Almost all language translation work nowadays goes through a stage of computer-based wordprocessing and in some cases Machine Translation (MT), and furthermore, clients frequently generate their input texts on computers and/or require translated output to be in the form of computer files to simplify further processing. Text delivery in the form of computer files therefore seems ideally suited to the translation business. Clients of translation services are often spread all over the world, and their staff frequently work remotely from home, so telecommunications seems the perfect way to deliver the information from computer to computer. Unfortunately, however, although these methods are now being used to varying degrees by translators, their application is by no means always straightforward.

The root cause of the complexity lies in the multiplicity of different and often incompatible 'standards' by which computers and communications networks operate. Differences arise at various levels which tend to make the business of exchanging a piece of text electronically between two computers on a casual basis many times more difficult for the user than, say, sending the same text by fax. Where different wordprocessing programs are used by translator and client, it is likely that many of the software commands in the files used by one computer (specifying font types, text position and table layouts, for example) will be unrecognisable, or worse still, will be interpreted incorrectly, by the other computer. Experience alone, often accompanied by considerable frustration, will show just how compatible two programs are. Successful exchange of text between different wordprocessors often necessitates using ASCII (American Standard Code for Information Interchange) files which act as a sort of lowest common denominator among different programs by stripping out all extraneous formatting features and saving basically only the bare text, but this obviously has disadvantages as some information is lost. A range of software products is available which convert files between the more common word processing systems, but complete transparency is assured only if both ends are running the same program.

Incompatible wordprocessing software is by no means a problem for translators alone – almost everyone in the business of transferring text between computers today will at some time encounter these difficulties. But for translators, there is an added complexity which few others encounter. The compatibility problems are compounded by the need to process texts containing diacritics (accents, etc. above and below the letters) and a variety of non-Roman scripts (such as Arabic, Chinese, Japanese and Korean) which do not form part of the standard ASCII character set.

Non-ASCII text processing

Computer processing of English uses the ASCII character set with 94 printable characters (upper and lower case alphabet, numerals and some punctuation marks) plus 34 other non-printable control characters (such as tab, etc.) There is also an Extended ASCII character set (which adds 128 symbols, but there are several different versions of this). By comparison, there is no single agreed character set used by Japanese computers, but at least four have been defined. JIS X 0208–1990, with 6879 characters, two previous versions each with a lesser number of characters, plus an extended JIS X 0212–1990 standard, with a total of 12,946 characters. In addition, computers processing Japanese recognise ASCII characters (or a near equivalent called JIS-Roman). The latest Korean character set standard uses 8224 characters; Chinese language computer processing in mainland China uses a 7445 character standard, and in Taiwan a 13,523 character standard. Every character to be generated by a computer requires a unique numeric representation encoded in binary digit (bit) form. Current computer technology is based on grouping 8 (binary value) bits into meaningful units called bytes which can take up to 256 different meanings (i.e. 2^8) – easily sufficient to represent each value in the ASCII character set. There is a universally agreed byte value for each of the 128 ASCII characters used to define any English language text (in fact only 7 out of the 8 bits are used; $2^7=128$), so at least when text only files containing just English characters and symbols are transferred between computers there is no ambiguity.

But when it comes to handling Asian languages, clearly an 8 bit byte cannot take on enough values to define the thousands of characters involved. For encoding Japanese script, several different methods have been developed, based on the concept of defining characters by a mixture of single byte and multiple byte units (and where either 7 or 8 bits are used), but unfortunately there is no universally agreed standard. Japanese encoding schemes include: JIS, Shift-JIS, EUC, Unicode and ISO 10646. Not only are they not entirely compatible with one another, there is not a straightforward relationship between these encoding standards and the four defined Japanese character sets. *Understanding Japanese Information Processing* (Lunde, 1993) comprehensively covers this subject, and is recommended reading for anyone handling Japanese text in an English-based computer environment. There is similar complexity involved in encoding Chinese and Korean. Furthermore, some of the encoding methods overlap, in that a particular bit pattern chosen to represent a specific Japanese kanji character, for example, may also represent a specific, and of course completely different, Korean hanja character.

Unfortunately in the English-speaking world there seem to be few computer specialists with a knowledge of foreign language computer processing, so many translators have had to develop specialised computer expertise in order to deal with these issues. As far as transferring non-English texts between two computers goes, many problems associated with interchanging files can be avoided if the computers involved are using identical software. However, in an environment where a translation company interacts with a large number of clients as well as with freelance staff working remotely, all of whom have access to a growing variety of software packages, this is very difficult to achieve in practice, and issues of compatibility take on great significance.

Modem communications

Another challenging area for translators wishing to send and receive work in the form of computer files lies in the telecommunications aspects. The basic requirements are that the computers which need to communicate must each be equipped with communications software and a modem. But unlike telefax, where the technical parameters involved in the communications are to a large extent fixed, or at least are hidden from the users and adjusted automatically within the fax machines, with computer communications users cannot avoid some involvement in decisions about how to set such characteristics as the data encoding method to be used, the transmission speed in bits per second and the error correction method. There is no single world standard for these parameters and rapid technological development means that equipment with a variety of capabilities is now in use. Further complication for international communications arises because North America uses Bell System-based modem standards while most of the rest of the world has adopted standards designated by CCITT V. series recommendations. When it is decided to transfer a file between two computers over a dial-up telephone line, the values of these and other parameters to be used in the communication need to be agreed in advance by the parties involved, and then set (usually by typing commands via computer keyboard and sometimes also by manually setting switches on the modems). This generally also means making an advance phone call to fix the time and details of the computer communications. Casual communication in this way is not user-friendly.

Electronic mail (e-mail)

A significant simplification in these procedures can be achieved if the two remote computers that need to communicate subscribe to an e-mail service. E-mail effectively provides a subscriber with an addressable electronic mailbox in a host computer network. Other computers can dial-up the network and deposit files into the subscriber's mailbox (using appropriate communications software and a modem connected to the telephone network). When convenient, the mailbox subscriber can similarly access his mailbox and download its contents to his own computer. By belonging to an e-mail service, the need to be concerned with communications-related parameters on a call-by-call basis is removed, as these settings are in general fixed for the subscriber's relationship with the e-mail service. Another convenience offered by e-mail is that the use of an intermediate network enables asynchronous communications between the two end-point computers. This means they no longer both need to be linked into the telephone network at the same time in order to exchange text – often difficult to arrange, particularly if the communicating parties are in different time zones. The economics of using e-mail versus paying toll bills for direct phone links between computers will of course depend on subscription and usage costs of the e-mail service used and the telephone charge rates for the distance and time involved; but generally, for long distance communications there are cost advantages in using e-mail. A great number of publicly accessible commercial e-mail services exist around the world, with CompuServe, America Online, DELPHI all based in the USA among the largest and best known. In Japan there are NIFTY-Serve, PC-VAN and ASAHI-Net, among others. With the soaring popularity of the Internet there have emerged many so-called Internet providers who offer e-mail services.

Two parties wishing to exchange e-mail communications do not necessarily need to belong to the same e-mail network, because many (but not all) such networks are interconnected with one another. Connectivity among different e-mail services is being extended rapidly to maximise the benefits of subscription. Internet addresses are beginning to become commonplace on business cards and letterheads – they generally take the form of the user's name, then an @ symbol, followed by a series of abbreviations strung together by periods. My own is: mohagan@taranaki.ac.nz. Whether a subscriber to a particular e-mail service can access a given e-mail address in another network will depend on the interconnection arrangements in place between the networks involved. At the time of writing, for example, the Japanese networks NIFTY-Serve and PC-VAN have both recently opened up links to the Internet. The ASAHI-Net also has international links. This may sound rather primitive in comparison with making an international phone call, but my personal experience with the system seems to indicate that an actual trial is the best way to determine whether communication can be achieved to a particular e-mail address.

If communication is possible, then the sending of messages in the form of ASCII text will be straightforward. Anything else can get very complicated. It is possible, for example, to send Japanese text via some e-mail networks outside Japan if it has been encoded according to the JIS standard and provided a number of other rules are followed. In some situations, however, Japanese text will be distorted by the e-mail process (which, for inter-network communication in the English language environment, is essentially designed to carry 1-byte, 7-bit ASCII codes) and it will be necessary to use special software tools to modify the text to enable it to be carried transparently (Lunde, 1993). It is possible for an Internet subscriber to send and receive Japanese language e-mail with subscribers of the Internet and other networks such as NIFTY-Serve in Japan. The peculiar rules I have learned by trial and error are, firstly, that each line length of Japanese text must be shorter than full length (e.g. 37 characters instead of the full 40), and secondly, in general when sending to Internet 'JIS' encoding must be used. International communications researcher and author Jeffrey Shapard (1993: 259) aptly describes the perils of electronic communications using non-Roman scripts as: 'treacherous waters for network sailors'. Similar challenges arise when attempting to transfer other Asian languages via e-mail.

In summary, although the extension of telecommunications to the exchange of written words directly between computers has brought considerable convenience to the language translation industry, procedures, especially concerning the handling of multilingual texts, are far from simple. Truly global and transparent communications awaits resolution of a number of standards and compatibility related issues.

POTS to PANS and VI&P

The advances in voice and text communications discussed above are just the beginning of the shift from POTS, a commonly used acronym for the early generation of analog-based 'Plain Old Telephone Service', towards digital-based multi-featured communications capabilities that will become commonplace in the near future. Gilder has coined the term PANS, meaning 'Pictures and New Services', to reflect the kind of services on the horizon. NTT, the giant Japanese telephone company, uses the acronym VI&P, for Visual, Intelligent and Personal, to illustrate its concept of the future, and predicts that with increasing machine intelligence and sophistication the extent of our communications will be determined not by technical limitations but by human imagination alone. The advances are expected to permeate both our home and working lives by broadening the scope of the 'who, where and how' of our communications activity.

One way of looking at the coming change to PANS and VI&P in summary form is in terms of this 4W1H analysis (Who is communicating, with What to communicate, When to communicate, Where to communicate and How to communicate) in Table 3.4.

Much of the enhanced development that will bring about the PANS/VI&P features is made possible by changes taking place in the technical infrastructure of public telecommunications networks throughout the world. Four important areas of change involve the concepts of Integrated Services Digital Network (ISDN), Intelligent Network (IN), Universal Personal Telecommunications (UPT) and International Value-Added Network Service (IVANS). These are terms frequently mentioned in relation to new telecommunications services, but perhaps not well understood, particularly in terms of how these concepts relate to new services and in particular services which have an impact in the language business.

ISDN (Integrated Services Digital Network)

Telecommunications services in the all-POTS era were characterised by analog transmission and switching technologies. Multiple services (then mainly just telephone and telex) were provided from completely separate networks all the way into each customer's premises. As its name implies, the fundamental concept of the ISDN is one of a network based on all digital transmission and switching technologies, with all services integrated and accessible to customers via a single line. The ISDN concept was officially approved by the CCITT in 1972 in the expectation that a proliferation of

Table 3.4 Analysis of the changes in telecommunications services

Attribute	POTS ————→————	PANS/VI&P	How (service example)
WHO	one-to-one	one-to-one	telephone, fax, e-mail
		one-to-many	fax, e-mail, BBS, database
		many-to-one	televoting
		many-to-many	audio/video conference
WHAT	voice only	voice	telephone
		data	e-mail, BBS, database
		image	fax, videophone, video conference
WHEN	at the time the call is connected	any time	voice mail, e-mail, fax
WHERE	at the fixed location where the telephone number is registered	anywhere	call diversion mobile phone

new communications services (enhanced voice services, data, telefax, video, etc.) would grow out of the developments that were then taking place in digital transmission, switching and computer technologies (Enomoto, 1988: 124). These were to be 'Integrated Services' because building a new network for each new service was seen to be inefficient from a telecommunications provider's point of view and inconvenient for users who would need different numbers, charging systems, and interfaces for each; and 'Digital' because that was clearly the way the world was moving, given the superiority of telecommunications systems that encoded information as ones and zeros rather than analog waveforms.

Today the Public Switched Telephone Network (PSTN), which enables one voice call or equivalent (e.g. G3 fax, or data using modem) to be made per analog circuit into a customer's premises, is still by far the dominant telecommunications medium used throughout the world. But behind the analog customer interface, PSTNs have progressively converted to a digital switching and transmission environment, using unit transmission rates of 64 kbit/s – the historical standard for digital encoding of 3.4 kHz bandwidth analog voice signals in the telephone network – under the control of digital computers linked by high-speed information signalling channels. Thus, the infrastructure for ISDN is now in place. It has taken many years to develop the complex technical standards, and then to build the networks, but today telephone companies throughout much of the world can offer ISDN capabilities via their existing copper cable reticulation into their customers' premises. And customers are progressively upgrading to ISDN terminal equipment, and gaining the advantages offered by the end-to-end digital environment of ISDN.

ISDN is finally operating in many parts of the world, including New Zealand, using unit transmission rates of 64 kbit/s. Data published in April 1994 (*Telecomeuropa's ISDN Newsletter*, 1994) made the following estimates of the number of ISDN customers connected in the following countries: Australia – 11,000; France – 144,000; Germany – 270,000; Japan – 270,000; UK – 37,100 and USA 956,000. And New Zealand had approximately 450 ISDN connections at December 1993, up from 50 at the start of the year (NZ ISDN Forum, 1993).

By dialling up one or more 64 kbit/s channels, an ISDN customer can send and receive vast quantities of data, representing not only voice, but any information at all which is capable of being digitally encoded. Common ISDN applications now in use include:

- Back-up transmission routes.
- Data/software file transfer.
- CAD/CAM (computer aided design/computer aided manufacturing).
- CLIP (Calling Line Identity Presentation).
- Group 4 telefax.
- Hi-Fi audio.
- LAN interconnection.
- Overflow traffic from leased circuits.
- PABX interlinking.
- Point of sale data transmission.
- Remote security monitoring.
- Video telephone.
- Video conference.

Some of these applications have specific relevance to the language translation business, and warrant further consideration here.

Group 4 telefax

As discussed earlier in this chapter, the G3 telefax standard which uses analog PSTN telephone lines has a number of disadvantages, particularly as a medium for translators to send finely detailed text. By comparison, the end-to-end 64 kbit/s digital path available with ISDN allows major improvements in quality and speed of fax transmission by removing the need for signals to pass through an analog stage. The Group 4 (G4) standard defined by CCITT for ISDN fax transmissions enables one A4 page to be sent in only about four seconds, compared with about 30 seconds for G3, while the output quality of G4 machines is similar to laser printer resolution and sufficient to reproduce the fine detail of some of the Asian language scripts.

British Telecom reports (*British Telecom World*, 1989: 35) that G4 fax machines were the first major application of the global ISDN to meet the increasingly sophisticated requirements of multi-national business customers for high-quality telecommunications. Practical examples include the British Library's use of G4 fax for high speed and high quality transmission of documents requested from users of their on-line information service. And in Japan, Takasaki City Office uses G4 fax to enable citizens to obtain various official certificates from service centres set up in train stations, etc. without having to visit the city office (*New Breeze*, 1993).

As with most new telecommunications technologies that require the parties at both ends of the communicating path to use sophisticated new equipment in order for either party to benefit, the initial adoption of G4 telefax machines has been slow, and their costs high, in comparison with G3 machines. But on the basis of past trends (e.g. with G3 fax, and even with the telephone itself!) as the quantity of new equipment in use grows, costs can be expected to fall, and at some point, a 'critical mass' will be reached, when a sufficient amount of the new equipment is in use to justify virtually everyone adopting it. Assuming this happens with G4 fax, then it is only a matter of time before translation companies find that their clients have upgraded to G4 equipment. When this occurs, in order to meet its clients' expectations on quality and speed of faxed material it will become a necessity for the translation company to also adopt G4. In doing so it will be able to overcome the problems cited earlier with G3 fax concerning resolution of text with intricate characters or small fonts as well as the time taken to send lengthy documents.

Video-based services

One medium of communications whose time has come, thanks to ISDN, is that of moving video images. Until recently, communication by moving colour pictures was largely limited to the entertainment/broadcasting business with its one-to-many communication relationship. Early attempts (Walsh, 1992: 27) to develop videotelephony (demonstrated at a World Fair in 1964) failed to gain popularity due to very high cost and poor technical quality, and attempts to market cheap, monochrome, still-image based videophones during the past decade have proved equally unsuccessful. One-to-one telecommunications remained a voice and still-image based medium, making it significantly inferior to meeting face-to-face. After all, seeing is believing, and a large proportion of human communication is said to be dependent on visual cues.

The time of the exclusion of video as a medium of real-time, one-to-one communications is fast coming to an end. In the past five years, major developments in picture compression technology (Fox, 1993) have allowed quality video images to be carried via a single 64 kbit/s digital channel – the basic building block of ISDN – and now videophones at a reasonable cost are becoming a reality. In fact, videotelephony is currently the major application of ISDN in New Zealand, and probably throughout the world (TUANZ Towards 2000, 1993: 8), with variants available which use one, two and six 64 kbit/s ISDN channels, depending on the required picture resolution and quality. Videophones are being integrated with personal computer terminals making simultaneous communications by voice, text/diagrams and moving video images from the desktop a reality. This is the world of multimedia. One specific application of video telecommunications that is now in regular use in some business and academic circles in many countries is video conferencing, which enables 'see and be seen' meetings to be held between people in two or more locations, usually in different cities, and often in different countries. Compared to a telephone call, the added dimension of image can convey a great deal of intangible, but valuable information. The economics and quality are such that while obviously not totally equivalent to being there in person, at least in some circumstances a video conference offers a realistic alternative to physically travelling to attend a face-to-face meeting.

It is this use of the medium that is likely to have particularly significant implications for the language service industry. International conferences are a major source of demand for skilled interpreters, and the shift to telecommunications based 'virtual' conferences will inevitably lead to requirements for interpreters to supply their services in the video conference environment. If such virtual conferences are going to replace real ones, then there will likely be requirements for text translation too, of the prodigious amounts of written material usually generated by delegates plus the need to cater for the real-time use of electronic whiteboards linked by telecommunications. Again, the issue of how best to enable the translators and interpreters to supply their services needs to be addressed.

Broadband

Meanwhile although first generation, so called 'narrowband', N-ISDN is only now starting to take off, work is well under way to define technical standards for 'broadband' B-ISDN. B-ISDN will provide users with variable switched bandwidth up to hundreds of Mega bit/s, carried on a new Asynchronous Transfer Mode (ATM) of transmission, and delivered to customers' premises by fibre optic cable. B-ISDN is expected to provide customers with unprecedented flexibility to access bandwidth hungry services including on-demand, high-definition TV and even 3D virtual reality games.

IN (Intelligent Network)

Underlying many of the new telecommunications services that are appearing today is the IN concept. The IN is essentially technology which enables part of the service logic for the PSTN and ISDN for a large area or entire country to be centralised in one location and accessed on a call-by-call basis. To appreciate the significance of this, it is necessary to understand that a telecommunications network includes switching centres or exchanges geographically distributed throughout the country, each providing circuits to a few thousand or less local customers, and also serving to interlink the exchanges with one another via long-distance trunk circuits. Calls are routed from one customer's line, via one or more exchanges, to another. Prior to adoption of INs, this process took place without any centralised control, as the exchanges were independent of one another, and so a call would be switched through the network directly in accordance with the destination address provided by the caller in the form of dialled digits.

The progressive replacement of analog electromechanical exchanges by digital computer-controlled equipment, together with the development of signalling protocols to carry control instructions to these exchanges in real-time, have provided the capability to add centralised 'intelligence' to a network in the form of a powerful computer, interlinked to key exchanges by data links. Termed the Service Control Point (SCP), such a central computer is the key to the IN. It receives information on a call from an exchange, consults its databases and sends back instructions to the exchange on how to handle the call, all within a fraction of a second. This makes service logic independent of switching logic and allows users to easily obtain flexible and customised services. Perhaps the most well-known IN application is the 800 number automatic reverse charge service.

When a caller dials a number with leading digits including 800, the exchange sends a message to the SCP with details of the call. The SCP translates the dialled number into a destination telephone number based on such information as the dialled number, the location of party making the call, the time of day, the traffic in the network, etc. and advises the destination number to the exchange which then routes the call. The SCP also keeps track of the call and arranges for the called party to be billed.

Other major applications of the IN now in operation in New Zealand and in many other countries include:

- **900 Number Services.** Whereby organisations provide information and services over the phone at a cost to the caller. The charges are included on the caller's telephone account and collected by the telephone company on behalf of the information or service provider. As at end of 1993 some 200 listed 900 numbers were operating in New Zealand, providing information such as weather and ski conditions, stock market reports, sports results and donations to charities.
- **Televoting.** Typically used to enable TV stations to conduct viewer opinion polls following political debates, talent quests, etc. Voters dial a number which corresponds to their voting choice, and the IN counts and reports results to the TV station.
- **Virtual Private Network (VPN).** A logical closed user group among standard telephone lines connected to different exchanges throughout the country, or even in several countries, allowing callers to use a special private numbering plan and to be charged special rates, as if dedicated leased lines were used.

Some of these current applications of the IN will impact on the demand for language services simply by boosting potential connectivity across language boundaries. Information supplied via 900 numbers in English only, for example, may well be missing out on market segments both in other countries and domestically, among populations of, say tourists and immigrants. An ability to provide information in the language specified by the caller could boost the use of some 900 number services. The IN may also become a key component in supplying language translation services via the telephone by providing the network logic required to route calls to human or machine interpreters when needed by customers, and automatically debiting the costs to the caller's telephone account.

UPT (Universal Personal Telecommunications)

The need for mobility in telecommunications has been clearly demonstrated by the popularity of mobility enhancing services such as call forwarding and cellular mobile telephones. Telecom New Zealand's cellular network has grown from nothing to 229,000 cellular connections (Telecom Corporation of New Zealand Limited 1995 Annual Report, 1995: 29) in less than a decade, and in the US, in excess of 15 million cellphones are in use according to the Cellular Telecommunications Industry Association (Langreth, 1994). The concept of UPT aims to provide customers with even greater mobility and location independence.

At the core of the UPT concept is the assignment of a unique, permanent telephone number to an individual, at which he or she can be contacted, anywhere in the world. The network will track the user's location, and will arrange to route calls to him or her, accordingly. Furthermore, all special services and features associated with the individual's number will be retained, regardless of which actual telephone he or she may be using to make or receive calls. In other words, the relationship between a telephone and its number will become completely flexible. The number will belong to the user, and it will be linked to a particular telephone (or other telecommunications instrument) only for as long as the user desires. It may change hour by hour, perhaps each time an individual moves from home to work, day by day, or be relatively permanent. UPT is currently the subject of intensive definition work by the International Telecommunications Union (ITU) as a planned future application of INs. But even before the international standards are finalised, versions of UPT-like services are beginning to appear.

AT&T's recent introduction of a '700' service is a case in point. It allows subscribers' phone numbers to follow them throughout the US continent, even when they are aboard aeroplanes with inflight phones where they can receive incoming calls. As with other telecommunications innovations, UPT aims to increase our connectivity beyond national borders; and this in turn will mean more opportunities for language service providers.

IVANS (International Value-Added Network Service)

While there is no agreed definition of what precisely an International Value-Added Network Service (IVANS) is, there is general acceptance that a Value-Added Network (VAN) is a communications network which is superimposed on a basic telecommunications network to deliver enhanced services, and that a Value-Added Network Service (VANS) is one which adds value to the basic telecommunications networks in order to provide a more cost effective service' (Bright, 1989: 5). Out of these concepts an IVANS has developed to meet growing international communications needs that are not fulfilled by national networks. Among common

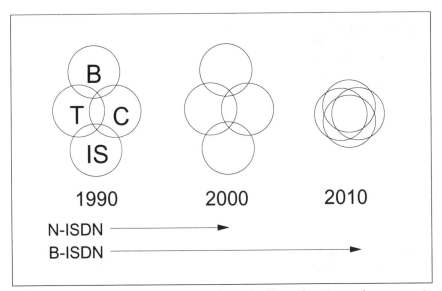

Figure 3.1 Convergence (Tiffin, 1990b: 189) of broadcasting, telecommunications, computers and information services

applications of an IVANS are Managed Data Network Services including
packet switching and protocol conversion, Electronic Mail, Electronic Data
Interchange (EDI), Electronic Funds Transfer (EFT) and information
services provided to third parties via computers and telecommunications. The inclusion of IVANS agreements (Cunard, 1992) in the GATT
accord demonstrates the growing significance of this arm of international
communications, the growth of which has been spurred by worldwide
trends towards deregulation in telecommunications and related industries, and the adoption of international standards. The IVANS concept
encompasses (Tiffin, 1990b) the merging of telecommunications, computers, broadcasting and information services (Figure 3.1 illustrates the
concept).

Early and well-publicised IVANS examples include SITA (Societé
Internationale de Telecommunications Aeronautiques) for international
airlines and SWIFT (Society for Worldwide Interbank Financial Telecommunications) for multi-national banking operations. SITA provides member
airlines with electronic links to aviation-related industries and transmits
transactional data, while SWIFT provides member banks with means to
transmit payment instructions in standardised form and messages on

international banking. Applications of IVANS are spreading to other sectors such as medical services. A remote diagnosis system using ISDN links between specialist doctors and their remotely located patients is in use in the United States. The system, which incorporates voice, image and data from various sensors, enables doctors to perform diagnosis as if having a face-to-face consultation. Extending such a facility internationally as an IVANS could make their expertise accessible throughout the world.

The provision of IVANS, however, involves complex issues regarding varying regulatory requirements, telecommunications standards and pricing, in addition to other difficulties involved in trying to set up communications networks in countries where telephone services may not be well established. As we move towards 'network-based societies' where a considerable volume of business and individual transactions is carried out electronically over the telecommunications networks, IVANS will come to play an increasingly significant role in future information service industries which trade worldwide.

The Internet

To conclude this chapter, let me return to the subject of the Internet as it demonstrates in a most concrete manner what the global network of communications is about. I limit the following discussion to aspects of the Internet which directly relate to language services rather than attempting to cover the subject comprehensively.

Shortly after the devastating Kobe earthquake in January 1995, a Japanese college student and keen Sherlock Holmes reader asked *Time* reporters to 'Please get on the Internet and notify the Baker Street Irregulars that all our members in Kobe are all right' (Desmond, 1995). Some people can hardly pass a day without accessing the Internet, even during times of major disasters. In fact, such out of the ordinary events tend to spur the use of computer communications. The Kobe earthquake prompted various cyberspace forum discussions to open up, and the computer network run by Nishinomiya City (mentioned in Chapter 2 for its MT service) which is located near the disaster area, quickly filled up with earthquake related messages and up-to-the-minute reports.

The Internet's popularity and the astronomical growth in the number of its users are well publicised; its influence is also indicated by the fact that its competitors like CompuServe, America Online and DELPHI in the US, and Nifty-Serve and PC-VAN in Japan, for example, have all considered it necessary to provide their subscribers with varying levels of Internet access. The Internet offers a rich variety of services including file transfer, e-mail, remote login, and a multimedia information resource such as the World Wide Web (The Web or WWW), which links related information using a hypertext structure, often with impressive graphics displays. Even audio and video conferencing is possible, while the recent introduction of facilities to make cheap toll calls via the Internet seems to have attracted a great deal of publicity.

Many of these functions have direct relevance to language service providers, with e-mail providing communications links to clients, remotely located translators and various databases for research purposes for translation, newsgroups, etc. One example is an electronic forum for Japanese/English translators and interpreters which was set up in March 1994 on the Internet with the main objective being to facilitate discussion of language and translation issues of common interest. By late 1995 nearly 300 subscribers were participating from locations all over the world with an average of 30 to 50 messages being posted a day. The forum epitomises the spirit of the 'virtual community' where people help one another out, and what's more, do so free of charge. Language professionals stalled over obscure technical terminology, cultural innuendos, etc. post their questions to fellow professionals, some of whom are bound to know the answer. The forum also allows people to advertise their own skills and jobs available. It is a highly practical and effective use of a global network by the people in the language business. There are also many culture-based newsgroups communicating in their own languages, often using the Internet's software utilities to enable, for example, text written in Chinese, Korean (Hangul) and Japanese to be read. This helps language professionals to remain in close touch with their specialist languages – the next best thing to physically visiting the country.

Although the Internet started as research oriented networks providing free information, more than half of the Internet traffic worldwide is now commercial and much of its increasing popularity, currently running at 10% to 20% per month, is of a commercial nature (Finnie, 1994a). For example, I've trialled a shareware version of a Japanese wordprocessing program downloaded from the Internet via FTP (file transfer protocol), a way to send and receive files to servers on the Internet. I liked it, so I paid the money and ordered a full version. This is an effective way of marketing a product by allowing potential customers to sample before committing to purchase, not to mention being able to do it all without having to leave the desk. New applications are also emerging with the Web used by businesses as an electronic platform for sales, marketing, customer services and a range of other front office functions (Finnie, 1994b). For example, computer companies use the Web pages to provide their users FAQs

(Frequently Asked Questions), fixes for software bugs, access to updated versions of older software and discussion groups about the companies' products. Federal Express Corp allows customers to enter waybill numbers for packages and get an instant reply on the status of their packages; and Canadian Airlines intend to provide real-time flight information as well as access to flight reservation systems (Finnie, 1994b). These developments can have a significant implication in terms of language service needs as the companies attempt to reach out to worldwide consumers using these tools.

With the development of global communications technologies and services, we can now communicate using voice, text or image, or all of them at the same time if required. Multimedia is fast reaching a wider community of people all over the world. Flexibility in communications today means the ability to keep in touch anywhere and at any time and is changing the foundation of businesses. As the opening quotation implied, customers may soon be advertising their requirements worldwide, instead of taking a passive role. The advancement of communications technology will see customers increasingly demand interactiveness, personalised services and ease of access. And this will likely include the means to overcome language barriers.

This chapter reviewed some of the technologies behind the global network of communications. It is now time to apply these new capabilities to provide and obtain language services in an appropriate form, where and when they are needed. The following chapter explores the symbiotic relationship which is now emerging between telecommunications and language services.

4 Marrying Language Services to Telecommunications: The Coming Industry of Teletranslation

> *In America AT&T is being successfully pressured to provide 'English-equivalent' phone service.... Dial a certain number, and you can do absolutely anything in your own language that you could do in English.*
>
> The Media Lab (Brand, 1988: 246)

Until very recently, telephone companies had nothing to do with language services. Yet the merging of telephone and language businesses should really come as no surprise. After all, both are in the 'communication' industry and in recent years telephone companies throughout the world have been diversifying their activities in response to technological, regulatory and commercial trends. Growing competition in the telecommunications industry is leading not only to falling prices but also to a shift of emphasis to 'quality' and new services. The sophistication of telecommunications technology is making the 'medium' increasingly transparent, so the quality of the 'message', not in the technical sense of clarity but in terms of its usefulness to the recipient, is becoming the central issue for both users and providers of telecommunications services. As a result, telcos are merging with computer and broadcasting concerns to provide 'enhanced telecommunications services'.

Converging technical standards and, more recently, corporate mergers, would appear to make it inevitable that broadcasting will soon integrate with telecommunications and computing on a number of levels. The planned merger of Regional Bell Operating Company Bell Atlantic with US cable TV giant Tele-Communications Incorporated, for example, would have formed an organisation with access to some 40% of US homes through the combination of the wired telephone and television distribution networks of the parent companies. Although this particular deal fell through, Bell Atlantic is investing heavily to provide interactive entertainment services (Kline, 1995). Rupert Murdoch's News Corp has acquired DELPHI Internet Services, which provides more than 100,000 subscribers with electronic access to computers all over the world (Rheingold, 1993). In New Zealand, Telecom NZ entered the newly termed 'infotainment' business by starting a cable TV trial project in 1993 with predictions that customers will eventually be given on-demand access to video libraries, databases and interactive services such as telelearning (Clayton, 1993). The move is seen partly as reaction to moves overseas by cable TV companies to supply telephone services via the same cables used to carry television channels, thus eroding telephone companies' traditional revenue base. Professor Negroponte, the Director of MIT's Media Lab, talks about the merging trend of telecommunications and broadcasting with a concept known by some as 'media switch' whereby telephones are increasingly wireless and conversely broadcasting is transmitted via cables. There is no question that the current demarcation among communications services will be progressively dismantled as the nature of the services themselves becomes a complex mixture of previously separate businesses.

These trends may imply that McLuhan's famous axiom, 'the medium is the message', is taking on a new dimension. In the new communications environment the media and services are merging as telephone lines start to carry everything that can be digitised. At the same time, this is making the medium less conspicuous; the user may not be aware of the medium as long as the message or the content is reached in the intended manner. For example, the time will come when your intelligent terminal recognises an incoming message to be fax, voice, or any other format and automatically adjusts itself to retrieve it. As the focus moves further into the content and as the marketplace becomes further globalised, the question of language barriers will inevitably arise as they prevent the message from being meaningful to the recipient. Thus advanced technical capability for worldwide communications is highlighting age-old language problems.

A case in point is a story behind the delay in Japan's adoption of the Internet. When the Japanese Ministry of International Trade and Industry (MITI) offered to provide Internet-linked computers to 100 schools in an attempt to reduce the gap from their American counterparts, it initially couldn't find any takers (Desmond, 1995). Officially the rejection came because the tight school curriculum left no room for additional material; but it is suspected that the real reason was to do with the lack of language ability to handle the predominantly English-centric Internet with ease.

While the Internet is regarded as a treasure trove, it is of very limited value to people without English language capability. Given that Japanese language based domestic computer networks are popular within Japan (for example, NIFTY-Serve has 870,000 subscribers as of January 1995), the use of computer network services could soar if the impediment of language barriers were to be removed.

This illustrates the growing relationship between telecommunications services and language demand. Language services are being called upon to make sense of the message when language boundaries are crossed. The logical solution is to provide appropriate language assistance at the point in the communications pipeline where the language problems occur. The past decade has seen the language business become a good customer of telephone companies, with telecommunications links progressively replacing paper and face-to-face contact as the interface with customers and teleworking freelance translators. First fax became indispensable for translation services, and more recently modem access has followed. Today e-mail is finally emerging on the horizons as a real possibility for language service providers. At the same time telephone companies have themselves started moving into language translation services as a diversification of their core business. So, whether it's translation companies supplying their services via telecommunications or telcos adding language services to their portfolios, there can be no denying that a symbiotic relationship is developing between these two previously distinct branches of the communication business. Such symbiosis forms the basis of what I call 'Teletranslation' – a service that uses telecommunications to optimise the use of language resources in order to provide translation of the written and spoken word. Furthermore, teletranslation has the potential to become an International Value-Added Network Service (IVANS) which will link the skill of interlingual communication experts and distribute their services, assisted by sophisticated computer tools and the instantaneous global connectivity offered by modern telecommunications. An IVAN Language Service is a communications network-based service which may be incorporated within public telecommunications networks. This issue is re-examined in the final chapter.

But today the relationship between telecommunications and language services is still at an early stage, and many aspects yet need to develop further if maximum benefit is going to be derived from this union. Building on the discussion of the current state of the language translation industry in Chapter 2 and that of the developments in telecommunications in Chapter 3, this chapter first looks in more detail at how specific new types of demands for translation and interpreting services may arise in relation to the development of the communications environment. For each case considered, means of meeting the demand is explored from the perspective of teletranslation. Finally, some specific examples of emerging teletranslation services are examined in order to pinpoint specific functions they are providing, their essential features and aspects which need to be enhanced.

Telecommunications-driven Language Demands

A major source of new demand for language assistance arises directly from the enhanced capabilities for connectivity offered by modern telecommunications.

By their particular nature, certain telecommunications-based services are inherently likely to create their own demand for language services. In other words, while new communications services aim to make people and information more accessible they also make language barriers between the communicating parties more prominent.

Telecommunications services of this type are summarised in Table 4.1, where they are classified according to the type of language service demand

Table 4.1 New language assistance demand linked to telecommunications service

	Real-time demand	Non-real-time demand
VOICE-BASED DEMAND	audio conference	voice mail
	video conference	audio information
	telephone	lines (e.g. 900)
TEXT-BASED DEMAND	chat mode	e-mail
	audio conference ⎱ on-line document video conference ⎰ exchange	electronic bulletin board
	on-line database (search process)	on-line database (retrieved data)
	specialised terminals	

that may arise. While most of these have been identified earlier in this book, I shall now consider them from the viewpoint of language service providers and identify how and in what form these services produce a demand for interpreting (voice-based demand) and translation (text-based demand), and then how teletranslation could help meet that demand.

Although Table 4.1 makes a distinction between voice-based and text-based services, increasing media convergence, as in the case of ISDN with multimedia capabilities, is tending to blur this demarcation from a telecommunications service viewpoint. This will affect the traditional definition of the work carried out by translators and interpreters, with the former dealing with the written message and the latter, the spoken message. For example, if a client wants voice mail in one language turned into written text in another, the process involves listening to spoken words and translating them into writing. Is this an interpreter's or a translator's work? This is one example of how the evolution of communications technology will affect the nature of the work of language professionals.

Tele-conferences (audio and video conferences)

Audio and video tele-conferencing are now supplementing and in some cases taking the place of physical meetings, as falling telecommunications charges lead to cost advantages compared with travel and accommodation. Whenever tele-conferences cross language boundaries the services of interpreters and often translators as well will be required, and these could be provided in a variety of different ways.

A very basic service would be for one or more interpreters to physically attend one branch of the tele-conference and perform consecutive interpreting on demand; but this would be barely adequate, as it would disrupt the flow of communication by requiring speakers to pause regularly while interpreting took place. Linking a remotely located interpreter into the conference via telephone would effectively give the same result; although it would have the advantage that the interpreter could be located anywhere within reach of a telephone, which would allow access to a greater human resource base – an especially important factor if highly specialised subject matter is being discussed.

A much more sophisticated arrangement would be to link the tele-conference into a full simultaneous interpreting facility of the kind provided at an international conference centre. Such a facility allows each participant to both listen to proceedings, and to speak, only in the language of their choice and without the need to pause for the interpreters. Each interpreter listens to the speakers' voices on headphones while almost immediately speaking the translated version into a microphone. Participants can hear their required language by connecting their headphones to the output from the relevant interpreter. To provide such facilities to participants in a virtual conference who are communicating over video and/or voice links would require some adaptation of standard tele-conference facilities, mainly to enable switching of each participant's communications channel to insert the relevant interpreter's channel. Such requirements are well within the capabilities of today's technology. While the standard 3 kHz audio bandwidth of the telephone network would be of adequate quality, the service would definitely be enhanced by the use of broadcast quality speech circuits which can be provided using ISDN 7 kHz encoding. Of course, in order to take advantage of this service, the participants as well as the interpreters would have to be connected by ISDN equipment.

In the case of video conferences, while interpreters could provide their services unseen by participants, exactly as they would for audio conferences, there may be value in providing them with the capability to monitor the conference participants visually in order to obtain cues from the speakers. This could be achieved by extending a video output of the conference to the interpreters.

The next step in sophistication is for the interpreters themselves to be distributed; perhaps working from their homes and offices all over the world and linked into the conference by telecommunications. A capability of this kind could be useful for both virtual conferences and traditional gatherings of participants at a single location, and further consideration of this kind of facility appears later in this chapter.

Conferences can create a demand for enormous amounts of text translation too, since participants typically need to exchange copies of their contributions, presentations and reports in written form. Today, fax machines and sometimes electronic whiteboards with fax transmission capabilities supplement tele-conference audio and video links to carry the associated 'papers', and wherever multiple languages are involved, translators are required.

Future conferences are expected to be multimedia affairs with each participant using a networked desktop computer terminal with text, voice and image channels all combined. Presenting a 'paper' will involve displaying text, diagrams and pictures on participants' terminals while simultaneously giving an oral explanation, and participants will be able to respond via the same media. Not only will simultaneous interpreting of the discussion be required, there will be an expectation that text will be delivered immediately to each participant's terminal in the language of their choice. In the past, conference participants accepted that requirements for translation necessitated their supplying advance copies of papers, and that translated copies of final reports would not appear until weeks after the end of the meeting. This is no longer acceptable in the faster time frames of today's and tomorrow's tele-conferences. Translators will have to find ways of combining human and machine resources to reduce turnaround times for their products to a minimum, and to link their communications channels directly into those used by conference participants.

Consider this scenario:

Medical experts on heart disease have voted to use ISDN tele-conferencing facilities for their bi-annual international conference in an attempt to reduce costs and time away from their daily work. Participants are equipped with desktop multimedia terminals which include video facilities and they have reserved language services for the duration of the conference. Each participant registers simply by dialling in to a previously advised number and inputting their password. As each 'paper' is presented participants see the text on screen translated in near real-time into their chosen language by networked human or machine translators. When the session switches to free discussion the video image of the speaker appears on the corner of the computer screen and simultaneous interpreters provide versions in other languages. Not only are the participants geographically scattered across the globe – so are the team of interpreters and translators, who, because of their specialised subject and language skills, have been drawn from several different locations.

Developing such systems will become increasingly important as the concept of desktop conferencing takes off. Price barriers will be a stumbling block if each conference requires an *ad hoc* network of language experts to be set up, but if there is a language service with already well-established networks of resources, costs may be competitive with international conference expenses, which include on-site conference interpreters and translation services. The availability of a readily accessible and reliable teletranslation service will greatly encourage the tele-conferencing option.

One-to-one phone calls

Many of the specific requirements for interpreting services that will arise from international phone calls will be the same as those discussed above

for tele-conferences that cross language boundaries. The differences are
mainly a matter of scale. Usually a one-to-one phone call will involve, at
most, two languages, whereas the international conference may involve
many. A large international and multilingual tele-conference, even in
today's high-speed world, is unlikely to occur spontaneously, so language
service providers will generally have some time to organise the necessary
facilities. Requirements to interpret for casual phone calls, on the other
hand, will arise at any time, without prior notice, often even part way
through a call, when communication difficulties arise, or perhaps when
another party joins in who needs language assistance. Users then need to
be able to draw upon language assistance immediately and easily, without
releasing the original call. The nature and subject matter of the call will also
have a major impact on the level and type of language assistance required.
Conversations restricted to very limited subject matter, for example, hotel
bookings, transport timetable enquiries and reservations, etc. are prime
candidates for automated language assistance. In the monolingual environment this type of call is already increasingly being handled by
computerised interactive announcement equipment that leads callers
through menus controlled by tone signals from push-button telephones. In
some cases speech recognition technology can accept spoken responses
from callers in place of tones. To expand services of this kind to allow callers
to use other languages in their interactions with the computer would be
relatively easy.

The January 1993 demonstration of automatic interpreting of a telephone call at the Advanced Telecommunications Research Institute
International (ATR) in Kyoto (described in Chapter 2) proved that
human-to-human conversations assisted by an intermediate computerised
interpreter are possible. However, the technology is such that, at least for
some years to come, interpreting of this kind will be available only for
conversations that are constrained to very limited and predefined subjects
and vocabulary.

At the other end of the scale of complexity lie conversations involving
detailed technical discussion, government-level negotiations, commercial
bargaining or social interaction, for example. Telephone calls of this nature
will continue to demand the services of skilled human interpreters.
Bringing an interpreter into the conversation via a standard three-way call
is technically simple, with no need for anything beyond existing telephone
network facilities, as this real life example illustrates:

> An import company manager in Auckland needs to hold discussions
> by phone with her suppliers in Beijing. From her experience of previous

face-to-face meetings she knows that the services of a Chinese–English interpreter will be essential if misunderstandings are to be avoided. She phones a language specialist company and a suitable interpreter comes on the line. As the interpreter subscribes to a standard 'three-way call' service from the local telco, he then easily extends the call to the supplier's number in China and establishes a call among the three parties – importer, interpreter and supplier. The interpreter handles the initial conversation and when the appropriate party is connected the interpreting begins. The importer asks a question in English, the interpreter listens, then repeats the question in Chinese. The response in Chinese is translated back to English. And so the conversation proceeds.

This is an easy, yet effective way to use a telephone service to help overcome language barriers. One important factor is that it makes the location of the interpreter almost irrelevant; he could be in the same city as either of the communicating parties, or in a different country altogether, just as long as he is accessible by telephone. The client can select the most suitable interpreter for the job according to criteria such as skill (e.g. subject specialist knowledge), price and availability. However, telephone interpreting using the standard conference call service as described above does have some drawbacks. As all parties hear everything that is spoken in both languages, the interpreting has to be done consecutively, say, sentence by sentence, and not simultaneously. This may be acceptable, even preferable, to some users who like to actually hear the voice of the other party, even if they can't understand the language, as the tone and manner of delivery can sometimes convey the speaker's unspoken messages. However, it imposes some constraints on the speakers, who need to pause regularly for the interpreter, and it lengthens the time taken for the process of communicating. By comparison, simultaneous interpreting, whereby the speaker's original words are heard only by the interpreter and the interpreter's words only by the other party in the call, enables a free flow of conversation. To deliver simultaneous interpreting to telephone users requires more than a standard three-way call, although it is within the capabilities of today's tele-conference technology. The speech paths of the participants would need to be split at the tele-conference bridge, and directed to the interpreter rather than to the other party in the call. One drawback of using the three-way conference call service in the way illustrated here is that the cost of the interpreter's services has to be invoiced separately. Despite its shortcomings, teletranslation providers should at least subscribe to three-way conference capability.

Voice mail

Asynchronous audio communication via voice mail has great potential as a specifically chosen medium of communication across language barriers. Unlike the immediate language assistance needed for real-time conversations, voice mail can be processed by interpreters, be they human or machine, in non-real-time when resources become available, as the following hypothetical example illustrates.

Suppose that our supplier in Beijing needs to get back to his customer, the import company in Auckland. Aware of the need for language assistance, but unable to access an interpreter at a suitable time to make a call, the supplier despatches a spoken message in Chinese to the importer's voice mail box. On checking her voice mail next morning the manager of the import company finds the message from Beijing, and by a few keypad commands from her telephone forwards it on to the voice mail address of an interpreter together with a spoken request for an English version to be supplied. The interpreter is alerted on arrival of the message, and as soon as time allows, retrieves it. He can listen to it as often as is necessary to carry out an accurate translation, and even easily copy it to a colleague for consultation on specialised terminology. The final English version is delivered by voice mail to the importer, together with advice on the charges for the work. If a response is called for, voice mail can be used again, with a message in English sent first to the interpreter for conversion to Chinese, and then on to Beijing.

While this example is hypothetical, it is quite within the technical capabilities of today's voice mail services offered by local telcos. Teletranslation providers should accommodate voice mail capabilities in their customer interface, not simply to answer incoming phone calls out of working hours or when lines are busy, but as a selected channel of customer communication.

Audio information services

Services whereby the telephone company, acting on behalf of the information provider, charges the caller for listening to information (commonly accessed by dialling a number with initial digits that include '900') are growing in popularity in many countries. Furthermore, with falling international telephone tariffs it is increasingly common to access such services across international boundaries. Foreign-sourced audio information implies potential language barriers, so service providers may have to consider language needs if they wish to sell their information into foreign markets. Domestic markets with large populations of immigrants or tourists who are unfamiliar with the local language also require consideration of language needs. Because this type of service most commonly supplies information in prerecorded form, this will usually mean supplying multiple voice channels recorded in a range of languages, and so will generally not involve a requirement for interpreters in real-time. However, as such services increase in sophistication they will become more interactive, for example, eventually incorporating voice recognition technology, which will demand more advanced language solutions. The audio information market may present a niche for a teletranslation, particularly for interactive services.

E-mail, BBS and database access

The practice of gathering information from databases accessed via dial-up computer networks is growing steadily, especially in the academic and business sectors, while BBS are popular among computer hobbyists. A huge range and depth of publicly accessible information is available, and by subscribing to electronic networks which have international links via the Internet, for example, information can be easily obtained from all over the world. But making databases accessible from overseas will inevitably mean either providing information in the customer's language or leaving the end-user customers to arrange their own translation. According to a survey conducted by the Japan Database Industry Association in mid-1993 (Auckerman, 1994), among 306 individual databases in Japan which are accessible from overseas over two-thirds (205) were in Japanese only, with the rest either bilingual or in English. And today for end-users to get such retrieved data translated would most likely mean sending the text by fax to a translation company after first decoding it from the non-ACSII coding (e.g. JIS).

Similar translation requirements will arise from a range of other branches of computer communications. E-mail and BBS, including the Internet's various forum groups, now enable researchers/students working on research projects to interact with their counterparts throughout the world, provided they all understand the same language. Or, if you have no time to go out shopping, a growing range of goods can be ordered from your computer terminal for delivery to your home or office. Teleshops enable orders to be placed via computer for items ranging from airline tickets through books, coffee and contact lenses to real estate, software and stocks and shares – by users who can understand English. The provision of translation services is a prerequisite for the expansion of these forms of communications across language barriers. A significant proportion of computer-to-computer communication of this type does not demand real-time translation; some delay in processing text can be accepted. For the ease of users with language difficulties some simple commands could be introduced for teleshopping to enable the ordering process to be carried out in the user's chosen language. Something akin to the automatic subscription systems employed by most electronic newsgroups whereby the presence of the word 'subscribe' in a message is recognised and triggers the subscription process may be suitable. But some activities, such as the on-line chat mode – written conversations in effect – can involve immediate interaction, and for these to take place across a language barrier it will be necessary to have a translator – human or machine – in the pipeline between the communicating parties operating in real-time.

Translators will find an e-mail address as essential to doing business in the next decade as a fax number is today. Some may wish to provide their services through third party computer networks, in which case they will need to ensure that this does not weaken the relationship with their customers. The issue of incompatible encoding schemes for electronic transmission of scripts which use non-ASCII coding will need to be addressed at an engineering level in order to facilitate the smooth flow of information through the text production process. Teletranslation could be incorporated into on-line information services as in the case of the CompuServe example mentioned in Chapter 2. The use of e-mail with allowance for different encoding schemes by a teletranslation service is essential if the service is to allow for languages other than those using ASCII-based scripts.

Specialised terminals

There is a growing trend towards the use of terminals in public places to provide specialised information and allow transactions to be made on a casual basis. For example, 50 'information kiosks', automatic teller ma-chine-like interactive terminals, are being installed in malls, grocery stores, etc. in Texas, USA, to provide such information as details of government jobs, unemployment assistance, etc. in both English and Spanish (*Wired*, 1994). Although we may not think of these as telecommunications devices, most are connected into computer networks which are in turn provided by telecommunications. Other examples include: tourist guides which display accommodation, restaurant and transport information; airline and rail timetable displays with the capability of making reservations and issuing tickets; automatic bank tellers which allow customers to query bank accounts and to transfer, deposit and withdraw money.

Suppliers of these systems need to give consideration to the language needs of their anticipated users. These systems are potential sources of language demand, as they all require the user to be able to interact with the terminal using the language displayed and they are all especially likely to be used by tourists. There is some evidence that language needs are already being addressed, as my husband discovered recently when attempting to extract money from an automatic teller machine in Hong Kong using his New Zealand credit card. Faced with a screen full of instructions in Chinese, he hoped he would be able to guess his way through the process successfully. To his relief, when he inserted his card, all instructions changed to English! Obviously the system is programmed to recognise the card's origin and to respond in a suitable language. Unfortunately banks in New Zealand are not yet offering the equivalent service for Chinese visitors.

Because these services follow a predetermined format, text in a given language can generally be stored at the terminals themselves, as in the case of the Texas information kiosk terminals. When services provide interactivity between users and remote databases they need to be connected to an appropriate language skill, human or machine, as required by users, to respond to *ad hoc* situations. As in the case of 'audio information services' voice-activated components integrated into these terminals will further enhance their user-friendliness which may mean the need for language service provisions.

Other telecommunications-based services

The marriage between computers and telecommunications is having an impact in a number of other areas with possible language implications. Education, for example, is a major growth market. Telelearning enables individuals to receive instruction from experts in a given field irrespective of location. B-ISDN Business Chance & Culture Creation (BBCC), an organisation based in Kyoto, Japan, carried out a trial of 'Tele-English lessons' using multimedia facilities based on B-ISDN in Osaka in 1994 (*Computing Japan*, 1994). Interactive communications systems are used to link teachers and students. The organisation will start the service commercially depending on the results from the pilot tests. To provide a wide variety of education in this manner will require language services in the communications channel between teachers and students. For example, piano lessons given by a Russian concert pianist to students in Taiwan will have to be facilitated by a Russian–Chinese language service. Entertainment is another potential market for language services, particularly as interactive TV and on-demand video become readily available. We may soon be thinking in terms of hundreds of TV channels to choose from instead of a dozen, and this will certainly include foreign language content. Calling up a foreign film which can be dubbed or subtitled on demand in your language may be a market for which a teletranslation service should cater.

Another significant sector whose business will be drastically changed by telecommunications is the publishing industry. *Time* magazine went on-line in 1993 (refer to Chapter 3) and nearly a year later UK newspapers *The Times* and *The Sunday Times* also launched an on-line service with DELPHI (Hart, 1995). The French daily *Le Monde* is already available on the Minitel videotex and is setting up pilot platforms with on-line service providers, cable TV operators and systems integrators (Hart, 1995). Both *Der Spiegel* (Germany) and the *Irish Times* are available on the Web along with Poland's *Gazeta* and *St. Petersburg Press*. Although European publishers are considered to be behind their American counterparts in terms of going on-line, the former has to cope with 'multilingual national publications and a myriad of telecoms markets' (Hart, 1995). Already we can read the latest Stephen King novel on Internet ahead of the printed copy, and books can be downloaded to our PCs to read on-screen or print out, as we prefer. Such on-line and on-demand publishing may boost new near real-time translation requirements if it is to access foreign language markets, and teletranslation will provide the solution. Instead of a lengthy delay while you wait for your favourite author's new titles to be translated some time after the publication in the original language, the translated version could be made available almost simultaneously with its first release.

Non-telecommunications-driven Language Demands

Of course, not all new demand for language translation will arise from increased use of telecommunications. But telecommunications technology can still help to meet demand from other sources in providing means to streamline the translation and interpreting process by linking the information source, translator/interpreter and information recipient electronically. As reviewed in Chapter 2, the key requirements for translation services today are speed, quality and low cost, and these demands are becoming increasingly difficult, sometimes impossible to satisfy without telecommunications links. The following scenario illustrates how telecommunication, combined with MT, could shorten the time frame for handling a difficult translation assignment.

A translation company in Wellington – in fact it could be anywhere in the world – receives an 80-page technical manual from a Swedish electronic manufacturer for urgent translation from Swedish into Chinese. Although this particular language combination is rare, a resource database in the translation office lists a number of translators who could handle the assignment. Because of the time constraints and the availability of domain-specific MT, a decision is made to have the first draft done via a dial-up MT system. Three potential translators are selected to supplement the MT on the basis of their language expertise and subject knowledge and they are faxed sample pages of the work. Two decide to accept the job – one in Auckland and another in Singapore. Their first task is to pre-edit the text for MT consumption. They receive half the job each, by e-mail, with initial instructions to prepare the text for machine processing by removing ambiguities and inconsistencies in the Swedish text. Within a day each translator has dispatched their pre-edited text to the e-mail address of a supercomputer MT system at the Carnegie Mellon University in USA. A few hours later a Chinese version is delivered to the translators, who then begin three full days work editing the MT output into more readable form. Next in the process is a subject specialist selected from the company's resource database. He receives the fully edited Chinese text by e-mail, then holds a three-way voice conference with the two translators and exchanges further e-mail to resolve some final points regarding the use of terminology. The final proofreading is carried out by a pair of Chinese native speakers who receive the text by G4 fax. The whole job is complete on the sixth day which leaves one day for the client's approval for particular usage of terminology.

In this scenario, the client's needs are met thanks to the immediate and efficient electronic links to the human and machine resources. While this may not be particularly futuristic, the use of the network services is totally formalised, avoiding the necessity of making *ad hoc* arrangements which eventually run up high communications costs and eliminating difficulties which might otherwise arise in coordinating each element in a coherent manner.

International conferences and conventions have always been a source of work for interpreters and also for translators. While the traditional gathering of hundreds of delegates in a single location may be progressively replaced by 'virtual' video and audio tele-conferences, there will always be a need for real meetings, if only to satisfy the human craving for personal contact and the experience of an occasional change of surroundings. Developers of virtual reality systems will no doubt accommodate these needs too at some stage in the future. Meanwhile, language interpreting will continue to be required when business, academic and government officials gather in person. But conference interpreters in theory need no longer be constrained to the glass booths of the convention centre. Today's technology allows voice links between delegates' microphones and headphones and those of the interpreters to be extended via the telephone network to any location in the world in the same way as described earlier for tele-conferences. To give the equivalent service standard of on-site interpreters would necessitate separate send and receive voice circuits to each interpreter to enable simultaneous interpreting to be provided. Existing tele-conference technology would be capable of achieving this. The switching of voice circuits between interpreters to permit the sharing of duties and regular breaks – essential in the high stress environment of simultaneous interpreting – is also quite within the capabilities of existing technology.

For voice-based services where there is face-to-face communication between a small number of people who do not share a common language, the need for an interpreter does not necessarily mean having an interpreter present in person. High-quality voice links to an easily and quickly accessible remotely located interpreter can be just as effective in many situations. Demand for dial-up interpreters on a casual basis will arise from the hospitality industry, including hotels, restaurants, entertainment establishments, etc. as long as the professional service is provided at appropriate prices and convenience. Suppliers of interpreting services in this form need to consider the practical logistics from the user's viewpoint.

A fairly cumbersome way of providing a remotely located service to enable two parties to communicate across a language barrier is to have them go to a telephone, dial up an interpreter and converse one sentence at a time, swapping the phone between each party. A significant improvement on this could be achieved by the use of a loudspeaking phone to enable the communicating parties to speak face-to-face, with the interpreter's translation being supplied over the speaker. An extension telephone on the same line or two separate telephone lines with a three-way calling service to provide the link to the interpreter would be almost equivalent, but probably less convenient. Finding one or more suitable telephones when casual interpreting requirements arise is not always easy, but the growing availability of mobile telephones will improve access to interpreters. When an easily accessible telephone interpreter service is available, there could be value in renting out mobile phones to tourists who are venturing into linguistically and culturally unknown territory and need language assistance as they travel.

Forerunners of Teletranslation Services

In response to some of these emerging needs, the past decade has seen several translation services come into being which have been deliberately designed for maximum integration with telecommunications systems. These are the first generation teletranslation services. Falling prices of telecommunications mean that language barriers today can form a much greater discouragement to international communications than does the cost of the communications channel. Translation and interpreting services that are easily accessible by telephone line can overcome language barriers and offer prospects for stimulating highly profitable international telecommunications traffic, and so several major telecommunications companies around the world now offer real-time interpreting services via telephone, using human interpreters. And computer network service providers are making translation services available to their subscribers who are increasingly venturing into unfamiliar linguistic territory in search of information or pure entertainment. Some of these first generation teletranslation services are summarised below.

Telephone interpreting services

AT&T Language Line, a subsidiary of the giant AT&T, operates a telephone interpreting service in the USA. Its origins go back to 1984 when a former police officer and a translator got together to solve a growing problem faced by immigrants and tourists – language problems when making emergency calls to police, hospitals, ambulance, fire services, etc. They set up a telephone-based interpreting service primarily targeted at the situation where easy and quick telephone access to language assistance could mean the difference between life and death (Qian, 1993). AT&T Language Line was formed with the acquisition of this business in 1990. It replaced the original old operator cord boards with modern telecommunications equipment to provide nationwide network services with a large pool of human resources. Although the service was established originally for domestic subscribers, it is now providing worldwide access. In the words of their brochure: '24-hour telephone-based access to more than 140 languages. Anyone can now pick up the phone and reach a professional interpreter from virtually anywhere in the world.'

Translatel, established in 1990 as a subsidiary of France Telecom, and KDD Teleserve, a fully owned subsidiary, established in 1986, of the parent Japanese international telecommunications carrier KDD, are both examples of similar telephone-based interpreting services. While the original rationale for setting up AT&T Language Line services reflects the multi-cultural environment in the USA, the mono-cultural situation in Japan explains why KDD Teleserve is almost entirely used for outgoing international calls by Japanese customers. For example, according to KDD Teleserve, 90% of its service traffic is between Japanese and English with over 50% of calls being made to the USA. It was pointed out that the users of the KDD Teleserve interpreting services are mostly private individuals and medium to small companies which are not able to afford a dedicated international section or in-house interpreters to handle international communication.

The following scenarios from AT&T Language Line are typical uses of these services (Qian, 1993):

[scenario 1]

When difficulties are encountered in a face-to-face communication situation, one party dials the language service number, specifies his requirements, supplies account information (credit card or special telco card) and is connected to an appropriate interpreter, all within a minute or so. Charging for the service begins once the interpreter comes on the line. The caller talks to the interpreter and hands the telephone to the other party so that the interpreter can relay the message.

[scenario 2]

Language difficulties are encountered during a telephone call. One party uses three-way calling to contact the language service, and once the interpreter comes on the line the two original parties communicate with the interpreter's assistance.

[scenario 3]

One party wishes to make a call to a someone who is known not to share the same language. The caller first dials the language service, and when the interpreter comes on the line, the other party is called using a three-way call. The interpreter speaks first, avoiding initial confusion for the called party.

While calls to KDD Teleserve are almost exclusively from native Japanese customers, the operators at the AT&T Language Line commonly receive calls from non-English speakers. For example, emergency calls in foreign languages are passed to an operator at the Language Line who must first identify the language in order to connect an appropriate interpreter. It is essential that the operator with whom callers have first contact is trained to interact to the extent needed to do this. The extended connectivity offered by such facilities as pagers and mobile phones enables interpreters for these services to work from remote locations, and allows access to a wide range of personnel. Interpreters typically work scheduled hours and are also available on demand to cope with unexpected peaks in workload.

KDD Teleserve's Ms Nakamura describes their services as 'value-added services created by combining modern telecommunications technology and human expertise'. She emphasises that the key to service success is having skilled interpreters who can convey nuances of conversation from subtle means of communication such as intonation and other elements which are by no means obvious. AT&T Language Line stresses the same point and emphasises the importance of interpreter training, particularly because telephone interpreting is different in nature from conventional face-to-face situations. For example, the interpreters are often unaware of the topic of the conversation, the levels of education of the speakers, and consequently their speaking manner, until they come on line. The interpreters therefore need the versatility to adjust to each occasion, often having to choose between providing a highly accurate word-to-word rendition of the original speech (e.g. in a legal negotiation) or conveying essential information only (e.g. in an emergency situation). One of the weaknesses of some of these services which is restricting their market coverage is in the area of billing. When local customers in Japan use KDD Teleserve, the cost of interpreting can easily be added automatically to their phone account. But when calls come in from outside the country charging is not so straightforward. Japanese travellers can use Home Country Direct and a telephone company charge card, but casual foreign callers face an inconvenient procedure of awaiting a return collect call from the provider of the language service who may otherwise not accept the request.

In summary, telephone interpreting services are catering for a niche market where real-time language assistance is needed in a range of situations, using the telephone as an intermediary. They have successfully added a new dimension to an interpreting service which was traditionally restricted to face-to-face and in person situations.

Translation services on computer networks

As discussed in Chapter 2, MT-based translation services are starting to appear on the menu of many commercially accessible computer networks, providing advantages of quick turn around and cheap rates, although the type of work they can handle is limited. For clients whose needs fall outside the range of 'MT-suitable text', human-based translation services are available via computer network, for example from the telco subsidiaries that run telephone-based interpreting services. Their sales appeal seems to lie in the extensive use of telecommunications facilities for receiving and dispatching work and also their specialisation in telecommunications-related text, drawing on the expertise of their parents' companies. One example of a translation company which makes extensive use of telecommunications to link with clients as well as with its own far-flung translators is WORDNET. What is new about the company is that it uses an Internet site to provide company information to prospective customers as well as to receive/dispatch jobs. It offers a worldwide translation service whereby a user can send in a text by e-mail and receive text translated into a specified language via the same medium. Delivery by most international e-mail networks, fax and courier, is also available, as required. The company has an extensive electronic database of professional language translators (1500 at the time of writing) classified according to language skills, subject specialisation, education, special training, special interest, etc. The database is critical to matching an appropriate translator with a given job. The company's brochure says '... if you need someone to translate that contract on delivery of respirators to Lima, we will find an attorney with knowledge of medical technology who is also a native speaker of Peruvian Spanish... ', and as any translation service operator will confirm, this level of service is just not possible without easy access to worldwide human resources.

A service designed to provide just such access has recently emerged on the Internet. It is maintained by Juma vof, Consulting and Translation Bureau in the Netherlands, and can be accessed free of charge. Aquarious Search System enables people requiring translation services to locate translators or interpreters specialised in specific fields and language combinations. It can also be used by translators and interpreters to make contact with their colleagues, and freelance operators who do not have the financial means to carry advertising costs can register with the system. It allows a search of a translator/interpreter by name, language pairs and geographical location. Once an appropriate resource is found, he or she may be contacted via phone, fax or e-mail.

In summary, computer networks can provide smooth and integrated front-end access to translation services direct from a customer's computer terminal while behind the scenes networks can be used to link worldwide language experts. In their current form, on-line translation services supplied via computer networks bring the major advantages of a smooth, continuous process for handling translation, simplifying further processing (editing, layouting, inserting graphics, etc.) of translated text and avoiding the need for an intermediate paper copy.

To conclude this chapter, a new translation service devised by Compu-Serve deserves a mention to mark the emerging 'teletranslation' services which reflect our progressively developing communications environment. In February 1995 CompuServe launched World Community Forum which includes near real-time translation capability by MT as an integral part. According to Dr Mary Flanagan, Group Leader for Natural Language Technologies at CompuServe, the unique feature of this forum is that separate but parallel copies of postings are maintained in English, French, German and Spanish, allowing multilingual communication between members who do not share the same language. This means that if a member logs onto the English version of the forum and posts a message in English it is automatically collected by the MT service and translated into French, Spanish and German. These messages are in turn posted to the appropriate target language forums at intervals of three minutes. Because the translation by MT is only of draft quality, the original messages are also kept to enable tracking when and if required. Furthermore, the system incorporates some specialised dictionaries to cope with discussions on specific topics. For example, a message in the Food and Wine forum will be translated automatically using the specialised dictionary in that field.

Special challenges faced by this application of MT are the extensive use of colloquialisms and the fact that writers often omit or misuse punctuation and capitalisation while including emoticons (e.g. :-)) and abbreviations in their text. In addition, the enormous variability in the nature of the texts makes it hard for MT consumption. Despite these difficulties, however, Dr Flanagan quotes surprisingly successful results: 'One member recently posted a message in English inquiring about hotel rates for his upcoming trip to Rangiora, Tahiti. Within an hour, a German speaker responded with the requested information. The response was posted in German and was quickly translated to English. In another exchange, a French speaker from Quebec seeking friends in America quickly received several responses from Americans. The English responses were translated to French, allowing the French speaker to communicate in French with Americans who spoke only in English.' CompuServe is planning to introduce on-line translation service into its e-mail and file finder services to provide quick, low cost draft translation in the coming year.

These examples demonstrate some of the changes taking place in the language service industry. The change in our communications environment is profoundly affecting the needs for and means of language service provision. Solutions are appearing in the direction of teletranslation; communications network-based language service, initially complementing and eventually replacing paper-based translation and face-to-face inter-preting services. For both the service provider and the user the next decade will bring an exciting and interesting development to facilitate truly global communication.

5 A Teletranslation Service

That [delay] was because the languaphone was working in real time. Sometimes there is no way to translate instantly a word's meaning, because you can't tell what the word means until you have seen the next word – like the words 'to', 'too,' and 'two.' It's the same with an adjective like 'bright', which might mean shining or might mean intelligent. Sometimes you may have to wait for the end of a sentence – or even the next sentence. So the languaphone, which animates the face, may have to wait for a complete expression before it can translate the Japanese speaker's words into English and animate the image to synchronize lip movements to the English words. The translation program works incredibly fast, but still it sometimes must freeze the image while it analyzes the sounds and the word order in your incoming call. Then it has to translate, again, into English. Only then can the voxfax start to transcribe and print out the translated version of the conversation.

The Turing Option (Harrison & Minsky, 1993: 16–17)

This excerpt from a futuristic story by co-authors Harrison and Minsky (the latter an authority on artificial intelligence) may seem a long way removed from today's first attempts at teletranslation, as described in the preceding chapter. And yet, if we consider the rapid advancements that are taking place in telecommunications, machine translation (MT) and speech recognition – the three underlying technologies necessary for such a 'languaphone' service to become a reality – Harrison and Minsky's teletranslation fantasy does not seem quite so far away.

What is needed is the integration of the component technologies into viable services which cater for the needs of the users – both customers and providers. This integration process is under way already in a piecemeal fashion. For example, the new 'Voice Foncard' service of the US telephone company Sprint recognises the spoken word as more user-friendly than a telephone keypad. It enables a customer to make a credit card call via an 800 number by speaking a 10-digit Foncard number over the telephone, into voice recognition equipment in Sprint's network, then simply saying 'call home' or 'call office' for an automatic connection to the appropriate number previously programmed into the system. Growing linkages between telephone services and voice recognition and voice generation equipment will mean that not too far into the future we will routinely have voice interaction with computerised devices when making enquiry calls to hotels, airlines, railways, conference and entertainment agencies, when transfering money between banks and ordering a pizza for delivery. Removing language barriers to services of this kind is well within the capability of today's technology. It would not be too difficult, for example, for voice recognition equipment to learn to recognise numbers and simple instructions in a range of languages, and to respond accordingly, thereby opening services to foreign visitors and overseas callers lacking local language skills. The increased use of these services in a multilingual environment will boost technological enhancements to speech recognition technology, which will in turn make linkages into MT systems to provide automatic telephone interpreting services more feasible.

But while a 'languaphone' may sound like the ultimate teletranslation service, it is by no means the whole picture. The wide-ranging nature of language needs, combined with the limitations in Natural Language Processing (NLP) technology, mean that human expertise will, for the foreseeable future, remain an essential component in a comprehensive language service. The role of teletranslation here will be to make this scarce and consequently expensive expert knowledge readily accessible when needed in economically viable ways through the use of telecommunications networks. And part of the function of such a service will be to allocate work efficiently among human and machine resources, on the basis of a number of factors such as time frame, budget, the nature of the work and resource availability. For a teletranslation service to achieve this will require attention to a number of design considerations, ranging from such detail as methods of customer access to services, protocols for text communications, work distribution procedures used behind the scenes by the translation service provider and mechanisms of charging for services, through to the broader issues of the overall structure of the service and how it all fits together. These practical issues are examined in the remainder of this chapter, which concludes by looking at some of the likely implications of teletranslation in our dynamically changing communications environment.

Key Attributes of Teletranslation

The following attributes of a teletranslation service are offered as practical guidelines to prospective teletranslation operators. Because teletranslation services could take any number of different forms and cater for any one or more segments of the market, some of these attributes will not, of course, be applicable in all cases, and an essential attribute for one business may be impractical or not viable for another.

Use technology to help customers determine their needs

First time users of a teletranslation service are likely to need assistance to determine their specific requirements. A senior executive encountering language-related misunderstandings in the middle of a phone call with an important foreign client is going to want immediate access to a human interpreter, with no expense spared. A research student who has just downloaded a dozen abstracts of scientific papers from an overseas database may be prepared to accept a low cost MT output delivered during the next few hours. There will be trade-offs among factors such as quality, speed, and price, as well as decisions to be made on input and output media based on issues such as budget, end-use of the translated product and the customer's IT environment, and customers will need assistance to select their best option. Confusion about customers' real needs often occurs even in conventional translation services in an environment that allows face-to-face contact between the service providers and their customers. The potential for misunderstandings in an entirely electronic communication medium is greater. It is therefore important that teletranslation services supply means of assisting customers to understand the services on offer and to select the most appropriate service to meet their needs. Ways of doing this could include:

- **Use of a front-end questionnaire**
  A predefined set of questions to be answered by the customer at a front-end menu, which may be either voice or text activated, could be used to help determine each customer's service requirements. For example, an Internet site via e-mail or pre-recorded voice system accessible via an '800' number could be used to provide this function.
- **Customer tutorials**
  Customers who anticipate becoming frequent users of the service could benefit from an electronic service guide explaining the full range of services available as well as providing tips to make the most of the service by citing actual examples.
- **Instant quotation service**
  Price will be of significant importance to many customers, so a means of providing an immediate quotation for work will be essential. Where charges for translation are based on number of words in the

source text a price can be supplied immediately from an automatic word count of text supplied in electronic form. Where special premium rates have to be applied due to the nature of the text, language pairs or urgency, etc., clients need to be informed at the beginning and the provider needs to use a fixed formula to enable a rapid and consistent response.

Provide a user friendly front-end to the customer's interface

Easy access by users is an essential attribute of any service, and language services which are aimed at a growing market in a rapidly changing and complex communications environment need to be particularly well designed in this regard.

A telephone-based interpreting service which has to be accessed by a deliberate action by the end-user needs to have an easily remembered, preferably very short telephone number. Secondly, the procedures to be followed by the customer after dialling the number must be simple, and here lies a potential problem. The issue is how to accommodate a multilingual environment at the front-end of the service, which by its very nature is likely to be accessed by customers speaking a variety of languages. Language services must avoid creating their own language barriers by, for example, answering calls and announcing instructions on how to proceed only in English.

Here are some possible approaches to the user friendly front-end for voice-based dial-up interpreting services:

- **Advertise a separate access number for each input language**
  Customers dialling the number for English will get all initial instructions in English only, and need respond only in English; customers dialling the number for Chinese can use Chinese, etc.
- **Advertise a single number for the whole service then offer a very simple multilingual 'front page' recorded menu**
  To avoid confusion, the menu would need to take the form of short instructions in each language, such as 'To speak English, press 1'; 'Pour parler en Français, poussez 2'. etc. After making the initial selection, all following instructions would be in the chosen language.
- **Advertise a single number for the whole service and have all calls answered by a skilled multilingual operator**
  This would effectively take the place of the automatic menu message and instructions to select the language by pressing buttons on the phone. If suitable staff were available it would probably provide the

most user-friendly option, but it would be very difficult to obtain the necessary human resources if the service aimed to offer a wide variety of languages.

- **Access the service using a telco calling card which includes the caller's native language encoded on the card**
  By making the service accessible only by dialling a special telco calling card number, or by using a public telephone that accepts telco calling cards, the front-end language to be used for the call could be encoded within the card number and automatically identified by the service. This is equivalent to the Hong Kong money machine example given earlier. The use of the calling card would also automatically enable the service to be billed to the card holder.

- **Advertise a single number for the whole service and use a computer to select the initial language based on the caller's voice**
  This is a futuristic option requiring sophisticated speech recognition technology which could determine the caller's chosen language by analysing the first few words spoken. Even such a system would require a language-proof means of prompting callers to start talking.

Maximise use of telecommunications services

Having addressed the issues of initial customer to service provider contact, the question arises as to what telephone services need to be involved in providing voice based teletranslation services. While a very basic service could be provided from a standard PSTN (Public Switched Telephone Network) connection and a telephone on an interpreter's desk, at least two additional telephone services are seen as essential to meeting customers' needs.

- **Three-way conference calling**
  Interpreting will typically be required between parties in two separate locations. While some customers may have the facilities to establish multi-party calls themselves, the language service provider should be able to offer to extend an incoming call from one party on to the third party to the conversation, so subscription to three-way conference calling is essential.

- **Voice mail**
  Not all voice-based service will be required in real-time. The fairly recent technology of voice mail is set to grow to become an important medium of asynchronous voice telecommunication. Voice mail could function as a useful 'catcher' of multilingual communication which

customers can in turn forward on to the teletranslation service. Teletranslation service providers need to subscribe to voice mail.

Beyond these two enhancements lie many other possibilities, and the number of additional telecommunications services that can be used to improve voice-based language services will continue to grow as the technology develops. The following capabilities warrant consideration:

- **Splitting input and output voices**
  Interpreting supplied via a three-way conference call has some disadvantages because all parties hear everything spoken, and as a result interpreting has to be provided consecutively. As discussed in Chapter 4 sometimes a preferred approach would be for the interpreter to use special equipment which separates the voice channels of the communicating parties so that each party hears only the interpreter's voice. This would enable simultaneous interpreting to be provided, with resulting savings in time.

- **Remote conferencing facilities**
  With the addition of special control equipment the interpreting needs of large conferences could be met remotely by a teletranslation service provider, eliminating the requirement to have interpreters on site at the conference venue. Video capability will greatly assist interpreters to catch visual cues from the speakers, and in future the use of speech recognition technology to deliver real-time on-screen display of the text of the spoken words would also boost the quality of interpreting.

- **Smart cards and speech recognition technology**
  In the future, applications of speech recognition technology and the use of smart cards will enable teletranslation to add new levels of sophistication to voice services, as described in the following scenario envisaged by Professor Nagao (1989: 144):

  > Each individual wanting to use the automatic interpreting system would be given a digital card which contains his fundamental voice parameters. These parameters would be permanently recorded on the card following a voice-recognition session during which the user spoke several thousand words slowly and distinctly into the system. When actually making use of the interpreting telephone, one would need only to insert the card into the telephone, where the voice parameters would be temporarily stored and the system adjusted to the idiosyncrasies of the individual's voice for private use.

  Credit cards and telco calling cards are already in common use, so a smart card-based scenario like this does not seem at all far-fetched.

Text-based language services demand equally straightforward customer access procedures which take account of not only the front-end language, but also complex issues of image quality and technical compatibility via a variety of media. Unlike real-time interpreting of spoken words, text translation will be mainly an asynchronous and one-way mode of communication involving dispatch of a document in electronic form for translation and onward transmission to a third party, or return to the originator. As such, text-based language services need a somewhat different approach to the customer interface to that required for voice-based services, and should include the following:

- **Provide customers with access via their choice of medium**
  Customers must be able to choose the medium of communication to be used with the translation service provider. This means teletranslation operators need to be able to receive input text in the form of a fax message, an e-mail message and via a dial-up link from the customer's computer. A comprehensive interface to customers would also allow for work to be delivered in a physical form on a floppy disk and, in spite of the technological advances, by paper copy. Similarly, the output translated product needs to be made available via any of these media, and not necessarily the same medium as used for input.

- **Offer guidance on the selection of medium**
  Customers may need guidance on the relative advantages of each medium of communication in terms of the efficiencies each offers for the translation production process and to ongoing processing by the end-user. For example, when a text is to be processed by MT a compatible format computer file is clearly the most efficient form of delivery. Fax or paper copy necessitates re-keyboarding or scanning by optical character recognition (OCR) equipment for input into the MT system, and these processes inevitably increase preparation time and lead to the risk of introducing errors. If the output text is to undergo further computer processing by the recipient, again a compatible computer file is the best form of delivery. Translated output which is required to be of publication quality is ideally supplied in the text format (including the font and style specified by the customer) suitable for electronic typesetting.

- **Offer G3 and G4 telefax**
  While the most common fax standard today is G3, which can be provided via standard analog telephone line, the ISDN-based digital G4 fax standard offers many advantages (discussed in Chapter 3), including the fine resolution required especially for text containing intricate characters or when refaxing of the same text may be

necessary. Service providers should be accessible via a combined G4 and G3 fax terminal, which means subscribing to ISDN, and advertising a fax number as G4 capable. Professional quality printing can be made directly from G4 fax output.

- **Advertise accessible e-mail addresses**
  Unfortunately not all computer networks are interconnected, or at least not yet, so for maximum customer coverage it may be necessary for a translation service provider to subscribe to more than one network and to advertise a number of different e-mail addresses. This can be further improved if different addresses can be advertised for different languages as in the case of Globalink on-line MT service (referred to in Chapter 4).

- **Support the required electronic protocol**
  As discussed in Chapter 3, computer-to-computer communication, especially that involving the transfer of text which uses non-ASCII encoded scripts, is fraught with potential incompatibility problems. Frustrating difficulties with the electronic transfer of text can be minimised if communicating parties predefine such factors as the character set, encoding method, and modem settings to be used for sending and receiving translation text. In order to accommodate customers' requirements, it is essential to have comprehensive communications software which supports all possible combinations of communications parameters.

Distribute work efficiently

In addition to bringing major benefits to the interface between language service providers and their customers, telecommunications will be the key to improved internal processes for teletranslation companies. The scarcity and rising cost of the multilingual human expertise required for translation and interpreting limits the number of language experts who can be employed on a full-time basis by a given service provider. Subject specialists and experts in rare language combinations whose services are required on an *ad hoc* basis will probably need to be employed only on demand, and this is where telecommunications can play an important role. Communications networks can be used to locate and then link up to suitably skilled experts, at virtually any location, provided they are in reach of a telephone line, and have the necessary terminal equipment. Once such an infrastructure is established it can be used to further advantage by also allowing full-time translators and interpreters to become location-independent teleworkers, for example, based at home. Indeed, through telecommunications it is possible for a teletranslation service operation to function entirely as a 'virtual' company, with all its resources distributed about many different locations.

- **Global resource database**
  The first requirement is for the service provider to be able to quickly identify and locate the most appropriate resources for each given assignment. Maintaining a reliable resource database is therefore essential. It should include information on at least the following attributes of each human translator and interpreter registered with the service provider:

  – name, location, electronic contact address;
  – relevant language pairs and specialist areas of expertise;
  – level of skill, qualifications, experience, translation speed;
  – availability (working hours);
  – text generation equipment (type of computer, wordprocessing software, etc.);
  – communications facilities (e-mail/fax/ISDN, etc.).

  The resource database should also include any MT systems available to supplement the human resources, including those accessible via telecommunications networks. In addition, information on editors, subject-specialists and any other suppliers involved in the completion of the service should be included.

- **Establishing the networks**
  Rapid connectivity with the required expertise is obviously essential, especially when customers expect services such as interpreting on demand and in real-time. Several of the recent enhancements to telecommunications services described in Chapter 3 can facilitate this connectivity. Remotely located translators and interpreters can employ mobile phones, pagers, and call forwarding and call waiting services to improve their accessibility. Intelligent Network (IN) facilities could be used effectively to route calls based on a time of day and language pair roster to appropriate interpreters who would provide real-time dial-up telephone interpreting. Conference call facilities will be needed by interpreters in order to provide their services in real-time, and they can make effective use of voice mail to interpret messages on a non real-time basis. Translators will need to be equipped with the necessary wordprocessing, fax and e-mail facilities.

- **Job tracking system**
  Task coordination among the various specialists involved in supplying translation will be particularly important in a virtual office

situation where expertise is geographically dispersed across several locations. To ensure a smooth work flow among translator, editor, subject-specialist, typesetter, printer, etc. systems need to be in place which pass clients' instructions to allocated translators and other suppliers, and keep track of job progress. This will help to avoid delays, as well as enable subsequent changes to requirements (deadlines, texts, etc.) imposed by clients during the job to be implemented. Like the example of Federal Express cited in Chapter 3, an electronic tracking system to capture the movement of each job would be ideal.

- **Job record database**
  This should include full text storage components and provide easy access to past jobs by providing an on-screen index, for example. The index enables past jobs to be searched by such categories as language pair, subject matter, client's name, or period during which the job was processed, etc. Each completed job would be archived in the job record database and be made available as required at a later date.

- **Training**
  To maintain required standards of quality among staff it may be necessary to arrange ongoing training, particularly as new services are introduced using state-of-the art technology. AT&T Language Line, for example, has found it necessary to provide specialist training to its interpreters who are required to be familiar with certain communication characteristics specific to telephone interpreting. Training of the interpreters or translators scattered in different locations could be organised, for example, in an electronic forum format.

- **Billing**
  Telecommunications systems can assist with the important matter of revenue collection too. Where language services are supplied as a subset of a telecommunications network it may be suitable for billing to be done by the network. Casual access to a telephone interpreting service could be via a '900' or equivalent number, for example, and charged to the caller's telephone account. Text-based language services offered by dial-up computer networks could, similarly, be charged by the network provider. Obviously charging should not commence until the actual service starts; enquiries and preparations prior to the start of actual translation must clearly be a separate component, provided at either no charge or a lower rate. The standard practice for telecommunications-based translation services seems to

be currently to charge on a per word or per byte basis, and for interpreting services on a per minute basis.

The expansion of services across national boundaries will make currency exchange rates significant, and teletranslation companies may be able to take advantage of variations. The huge discrepancies in international telephone call tariffs will also make the issue of originating country of a call important to teletranslation service providers.

Bringing It All Together

At a macro level, a future teletranslation service must be considered as one component of a highly information and telecommunications oriented society in which all kinds of information in electronic form are traded internationally. Such an information society is likely to undergo progressive development. Its precise shape at any given time in the future cannot be easily predicted, but in the view of Kapor, who started the Electronic Frontier Foundation (EFF), and Weitzner, the main channels for commerce, education and entertainment in future will be 'the international public network (IPN)... an interconnected confederation of numerous networks' (Kapor & Weitzner, 1993: 300) which extend throughout the world. It is in this environment that teletranslation will thrive as an International Value-Added Network Service (IVANS).

A growing number of businesses such as airlines, banks and couriers are taking advantage of streamlined cross-border communications links for their day-to-day operations to capture information in the most efficient and cost-effective manner. During the next decade today's industry-based closed IVANS may be extended to networks open to the general public. Given the push towards information superhighways and the exponential growth seen in computer network services, IVANS are likely to constitute the backbone of the information services in the coming decade. Without discounting the bottlenecks expected to affect the further developments of IVANS, including regulatory issues, the discrepancies in telecommunications standards and in the level of facilities available in different countries, there are nonetheless clear indications that the increasing need for global information pipelines will force introduction of new clusters of IVANS. Given the rising demand and technical feasibility, the establishment of 'Language IVANS', along with Medical IVANS (as referred to in Chapter 3), Educational IVANS, Tourism IVANS, etc. may be possible.

A language IVANS will exploit the power of the international public network to link the specialised skills of translators and interpreters with related functions such as terminology databases, electronic typesetting, printing, publishing and distribution systems, for example, making a full range of related resources available through a single 'one-stop shop' network. The larger the scale of the network and the wider the scope of interconnectivity among different groups of IVANS (for example, Language IVANS may be combined with Tourism IVANS), the more cost-effective and comprehensive the resulting services will become.

One vision of how teletranslation will fit into the information infrastructure early next century is that of the Japanese telecommunications provider NTT, which sees a language service as a new and important feature of their future telecommunications services and as very much part of their forward planning (NTT Gijutsu Doko Kenkyukai, 1990). Their 'VI&P' (Visual, Intelligent and Personal) service vision for the 21st century (discussed briefly in Chapter 3) envisages a language service integrated within its 'Intelligent' communications services, with NLP technology added to their telephone networks to perform automatic translations of text and speech. NTT describes its vision as follows:

> There will still be language barriers in the 21st century. Text translation services will be available via telecommunications whereby input texts are processed by automatic translation functions built-in to the network. Such services will initially be targeted at corporate users and gradually be extended to the needs of private individuals. They will include display of the original input text along with the translated text, and output of the translated text in the form of a synthetic voice. Users will be able to select the most suitable service according to their needs. Interpreting telephony which recognizes a spoken message, translates it automatically into another language and outputs it as a synthetic voice to the recipient will be the next step. Realization of these services will be made possible by new telecommunications systems, making world communication easier in the 21st century. (NTT Gijutsu Doko Kenkyukai, 1990: 188)

The major advantage of the language service being provided by a telecommunications carrier is seen as being its full integration into the public communications networks, making customer access seamless. For example, users could add interpreting services to their calls simply by dialling extra digits which would automatically route them to computer-based interpreting assistance for the selected language. Or for text-based services, an e-mail message may be directed to the intended destination via

Figure 5.1 NTT's concept of intelligent service – tele-banquet (Suzuki, 1993)

an appropriate text translation service, again simply by the addition of a code to the normal e-mail address. Charging for the service could be easily incorporated into the subscriber's telephone bill.

NTT considers overcoming linguistic and cultural barriers as an important challenge for future telecommunications technology. It envisages the 'virtual' banquet scene of Figure 5.1 held via telecommunications network, connecting people in three separate locations, speaking French, English and Japanese, with conversation automatically translated into the appropriate languages while realistic images on 3-D screens provide a sense of proximity.

NTT's vision demonstrates the enormous potential of teletranslation to become an integral part of our standard communications network services. The media convergence currently in progress will give subscribers access to voice, text and pictures via a single terminal. This means that the world of cyberspace will be integrated into standard telephone services. Current technological trends suggest that the information superhighway will eventually become accessible to a large proportion of the world's population, forming something akin to the concept of the IPN. This is the time for electronic commerce or IVANS to replace the conventional way of trading and any other activities which can be represented in digital signals and involve worldwide information exchange. In this picture, globally accessible teletranslation will become an essential ingredient.

The greatest breakthrough in the language service industry during the last five years has come from the capability of communications networks. Today translation services cannot function without fax and electronic data links which form the core interface with customers and also with teleworking freelance translators. While computer technologies such as multilingual wordprocessors and DTP (desktop publishing) greatly enhanced the productivity in the translation office, their effectiveness was even greater when combined with telecommunications. The same formula is starting to be applied to MT and speech recognition technologies as they are integrated into communications networks. The development of teletranslation will not be dependent on the degree of perfection MT may attain, but will be critically influenced by how global communications networks evolve. In other words, whether or not a tele-banquet is facilitated by human interpreters or machine counterparts is a secondary issue. What is important is that when telephone companies start delivering a 'virtual international meeting' service such as this, suitable language assistance facilities will be essential. Without the marriage of language services and telecommunications to create teletranslation such services cannot hope to become truly international.

Implications

Eliminating language barriers seems to be one of the last technical challenges left to modern communications technologies, and in this book I have endeavoured to describe what is beginning to happen in the field of language services and introduce the emerging change as a teletranslation service. I have also indicated that the creation of an advanced teletranslation service is related to developments of: (1) increasingly well designed and densely connected reliable communications networks;and (2) a breakthrough in NLP or specifically MT technology. Within each of these areas there are a number of significant implications which are associated with the introduction of a teletranslation service:

Global networks and language businesses

Today a large number of freelance translators are working remotely using fax, PC and modem. These individuals are starting to take advantage of technology to become global teleworkers, working for various translation firms and directly for customers in diverse locations all over the world.

In the wake of more IT-astute organisations which were quick to adopt data communications via LANs and WANs, language businesses have started to use modems to communicate with translators and clients. Language service providers are now in a transitional period of partially exploiting the new communications realm by using e-mail and the Internet. An e-mail address is starting to be seen by geographically spread customers as a more functional window for access than a telephone, fax or modem number. Translators are also taking advantage of electronic forums run on global networks to seek advice from a large number of colleagues via a single message posted to the forum.

Soon skilled translators and interpreters will be working for a number of teletranslation services, instantly multiplying their job opportunities and at the same time sharing knowledge with far-flung networked translators. Possible issues to arise from this type of working arrangement may then be the discrepancies in professional fees from country to country, involving such factors as currency exchange rates and international telecommunications tariffs. Also, as the use of networks becomes more formalised and commercially oriented, the goodwill 'forum' discussions may be discouraged where the information exchanged is considered as too valuable or of a proprietary nature. Another concern is information overload caused when the number of members in one forum goes beyond a manageable level so the number of postings exceeds what each participant is capable of receiving and reading. The forum I belong to has average postings of 30–50 messages a day, for example, and if this number doubles it will start hindering rather than helping my work.

Other issues which may need to be addressed stem from new communication behaviours arising in cyberspace. It has been well recognised by users of the medium that because e-mail messages take a form which is closer to spoken rather than written language, yet without facial or vocal cues, incidents of friction and misunderstanding, known as 'flaming' within the network community, can arise. A code of ethics called 'netiquette' has been developed to help users to reduce the incidence of these undesirable results. Such negative impacts of the use of networks have to be taken into account.

One of the first publications to deal with such subjects, *Global Networks* (Harasim, 1993), explores the present and the future course of a network-based society and is itself evidence of the revolution in progress. The book was put together by multi-authoring via computer networks, connecting authorities in each field from all over the world. Hyper-authoring, as some call this way of writing, provides authors with a new kind of environment where one person's viewpoint can be aired instantly to many others in different physical locations, often with immediate feedback. This provides a useful tool for the author and the editor, for example, where frequent feedback during the process of writing means subsequent time-saving for the editing procedure. As a subcategory of hyper-authoring, hyper-translating, where a number of translators are linked over distance on computer networks during the translating process, is also starting to emerge.

A Japanese version of Mark Poster's *Mode of Information* (which examines the relationship between cyberspace and poststructuralism) was produced in this manner with two translators who were linked via computer network with each assigned different chapters to translate. One of the translators commented (Poster, 1991: 308) that because the translated text was being swapped between them during the translation process, the text gathered a somewhat collective identity. This is strikingly different from the normal translation process which tends to absorb the translator who becomes identified with the translated text. How this will affect the quality of the resulting translation is an open question, and will make an interesting topic for future research.

MT and language businesses

The application of IT to the qualitative rather than the quantitative aspect of our information processing activities has earned labels such as 'intelligent' technology. MT can be considered as one such technology which is going to make a major impact on the translation industry in the coming decades.

As seen in the application of MT combined into computer networks, it seems very likely that before very long the general public will become more regularly exposed to MT outputs, whereas so far MT has mainly been used behind the scenes by language professionals. One of the implications of the increased use of MT in future is that we will probably start to accept and become accustomed to less than perfect translations with slightly unidiomatic expressions or perhaps awkward ways of expressing ideas, as long as they serve the purpose of a given communicative situation. In combination with speech recognition technology, MT will facilitate voice interaction across language barriers, even though it may at first seem extremely crude. However, the capability of telecommunications systems to carry images may partially compensate for this by providing visual cues such as facial expressions and body language. New applications of NLP technology have to be explored from the point of view of communication as a whole.

There is no doubt that the NLP developments will lead to drastic changes within and outside the translation industry. Firstly a stronger presence of MT will affect the nature of the client's needs and expectations for language services. Readily available and inexpensive PC-based MT software products could permanently eliminate a certain segment of the potential translation market, leading to more clearly defined roles developing for MT and its human counterpart. At present, MT needs to have a 'tailored environment' to work effectively and therefore its main applications are for technical 'domain-specific' documents. Another use may be possible where MT performs a 'general practitioner' role or a first pass, to provide an initial diagnosis of the translation task and determine the degree of 'translatability' or difficulty of the text, for example. In any case there will be no escaping the fact that human translators must be prepared to co-exist with MT in various ways in the coming decade.

The implications of MT on language learning may also be significant. Will widespread use of MT eliminate the incentive to learn languages? So far the increased opportunities to encounter different cultures and languages seem to have encouraged a desire for language learning. While readily available language aids such as a teletranslation service may fully satisfy immediate language needs, the availability of new learning opportunities such as 'tele-lessons' direct from the country where the learner's choice of language is spoken may greatly encourage language learning. MT itself could be used as an aid to learning languages by providing interactive lessons tailored to suit individual students' needs.

While so-called 'intelligent technologies' such as NLP may provide us with cheaper and more convenient language services, there are dangers in over reliance on automatic translating machines. For example, naive users of cut-rate automatic interpreting telephony may suffer from critical misunderstandings caused by unexpected machine errors. This may not only be a matter of losing subtle nuances in the message, but involve crass mistakes such as reversing positive to negative answers, which would inevitably invite disastrous consequences. Both users and providers of the service will have to approach these supposedly intelligent technologies with considerable caution and allowance for errors. For this reason, no matter how 'intelligent' technology may become, human expertise is likely to remain important if only as an occasional helper.

Whether and when a comprehensive teletranslation service will become a reality depends on the attitude we take now and on our vision of the future. It will require cooperation particularly between the currently separate industries of language and telecommunications. Their integration will be essential to the realisation of true 'Global Communication', not only in the technical sense of connectivity, but in achieving meaningful communication between people who speak different languages. I welcome the forthcoming marriage between the language and telecommunications industries, and look forward to greeting the progeny of this union – a vigorous healthy teletranslation service.

Epilogue

The rationale for creating a teletranslation service is essentially to connect appropriate human or machine expertise to individuals requiring language assistance in a timely and cost-effective manner. Well designed communications networks can facilitate this function in real-time and on a global scale. Perhaps the following scenario may give some idea of how an advanced teletranslation service of the future may function:

March 2020, a holiday house in the Japanese countryside. An executive sits at his desk overlooking the blue ocean, pondering over his investment in a South Pacific hotel chain. Deciding he needs more information, Mr Tanaka asks his broadband ISDN terminal to connect him to his New Zealand area manager, Mr Hone. The voice recognition system processes the spoken instructions and Hone's personal communications number is retrieved from the terminal's memory and dialled. Within seconds, super-intelligent network systems in Japan and New Zealand locate the Kiwi businessman en-route to Auckland aboard a domestic flight, and arrange a connection to the audiovisual terminal in the seat armrest, into which Hone had inserted his personal identity card at the beginning of the flight. Knowing his Japanese is not up to conducting serious business discussions, after exchanging a few words of greeting Hone asks his caller to stand by a moment. By punching a few digits into the terminal he requests the services of a teleinterpreter, selecting 'high level assistance' as accuracy is of paramount importance in this instance. From its resource database of several hundred interpreters multi-national teletranslation company Babeltel selects Yuriko in Wellington to do the job, and links her terminal into the conversation. She immediately ceases her keyboarding work, dons headphones and signals she is ready to go.

In less than half a minute Tanaka is listening to Yuriko, electronically modulated to a male voice, giving Hone's enthusiastic report of the latest room occupancy figures, all in immaculate Japanese. Behind the scenes Yuriko is speaking via her intelligent terminal, interpreting Hone's words into Japanese and Tanaka's into English. Her work quality and efficiency are enhanced by the top quality digital voice channel, the built-in speech recognition system displaying the written rendition of the spoken messages, and her immediate access to a voice-activated on-line dictionary. As a teleworker, her clients have no idea where she is actually located; Babeltel's database system allocates jobs to the most suitable available language experts, depending on location, language pair and speciality.

By the way, Tanaka no longer has to face language problems ordering room service when he visits Auckland. The guest rooms in his hotels are all equipped with interactive multilingual terminals capable of handling requests in different languages, and for more complex transactions, Babeltel's access number is preprogrammed into the ISDN telephone in each room.

Exactly when this level of refinement is reached remains a question, but there can be no doubt that teletranslation services will continue to help close communication gaps which would otherwise be widening as we move towards the new communications age. It is also apparent that different varieties of teletranslation, quite beyond our present imaginations, will emerge to satisfy our ever changing communications needs. They will encourage monolingual individuals to make more use of international telecommunications and to maximise and enjoy new activities in cyber-space. This is when the global village will truly be transformed into a space unhindered by language barriers.

Glossary of Terms

American Standard Code for Information Interchange (ASCII) A standard computer character set comprising 128 characters used to enable data communication between computers.

Artificial Intelligence (AI) Computer programs which attempt to imitate human functions of reasoning, inference, recognition, learning, etc.

Asynchronous Transfer Mode (ATM) A technology to enable digital signals of different speeds, such as for voice and image, to be transmitted over one conduit. ATM is the means of delivering Broadband ISDN.

Audio Conference Telephone service which allows individuals in three or more separate locations to talk to one another.

Bit Binary digit. Smallest piece of information, with values or states of 0 or 1, or yes or no, used as the basis of digital computer processing and information storage.

Broadband Integrated Services Digital Network (B-ISDN) See ISDN.

Bromide A photograph of a printed page used by printers to prepare a printing plate.

Bulletin Board System (BBS) Networked computer terminals which enable individuals to communicate, share files and access information.

Byte A grouping of (often, but not necessarily 8) bits operating together.

Cellular Telephone A wireless telephone system that operates within a grid of radio sender-receivers. As a user moves to different locations on the grid, different receiver-transmitters automatically support the message traffic.

Chat Also known as talk. Real-time on-screen dialogues carried out by typing between parties connected via computer networks.

Consultative Committee for International Telephone and Telegraph (CCITT) Former arm of the ITU which established telecommunications standards. The activities of CCITT are now done within the ITU itself.

Cyberspace The communications space or world created by interlinked computers.

Desktop Publishing (DTP) A computer application to streamline the process of creating documentation, including sophisticated graphics via desktop computer.

Electronic Data Interchange (EDI) Electronic exchange of structured information (usually business documentation) over a computer network.

Electronic Funds Transfer (EFT) Electronic payment where transfer of money between bank accounts is automatic.

Electronic Mail (E-Mail) A means to store and deliver messages including graphics electronically by interconnected computers.

Emoticon ASCII symbols used to give graphical display of emotions. For example :-) to indicate a smile.

Facsimile, fax See telefax.

File Transfer Protocol (FTP) The Internet standard protocol for transferring files from one computer to another.

G3 fax Group 3 telefax. The most commonly used facsimile standard that operates over analog telephone lines.

G4 fax Group 4 telefax. A new generation facsimile standard used via ISDN or private digital circuits, providing far superior speed and resolution compared with G3.

Gopher An information retrieval system developed at the University of Minnesota to facilitate ease of accessing information on the Internet.

Hypermedia An information storage and retrieval system whereby information often with images can be accessed by following the links embedded in a document.

Information Superhighway A term coined by the US Vice President Al Gore which refers to new high capacity information networks.

Integrated Services Digital Network (ISDN) A public telecommunications network that provides a multiplicity of services via a single high-speed digital connection to the user. First generation ISDN, based on 64 kbit/s transmission, is now known as Narrowband (N-ISDN). Second generation ISDN, based on ATM, is known as Broadband (B-ISDN).

International Telecommunications Union (ITU) A world body that produces technical standards for telecommunication.

International Value-Added Network Service (IVANS) Enhanced telecommunications service provided internationally over and above basic voice services.

Internet A confederation of many individual networks connected via TCP/IP protocols.

Interpreter A person who translates a spoken message in one natural language into a spoken message into another. The interpreting style may be either consecutive or simultaneous. The latter is often used for international conferences.

Japanese Industrial Standard (JIS) The standards established by Japanese Industrial Standards Committee (JISC).

Local Area Network (LAN) Special linkage of computers or other communications devices into their own network for use by an individual or organisation.

Machine Translation (MT) A computer program to translate text written in one natural language into another.

Modem Modulator-demodulator. Equipment used to link a computer to a telephone line.

Multimedia Computer system which presents information via different media such as voice, text and picture.

Narrowband Integrated Services Digital Network (N-ISDN) See ISDN.

Natural Language Processing (NLP) A computer application to process the same written or spoken language as used by humans (i.e. natural language). MT can be seen as a subset of NLP.

Optical Character Recognition (OCR) A technology used to scan and convert written characters into digital format, enabling further processing.

Plain Old Telephone Service (POTS) Basic telephone service.

Public Switched Telephone Network (PSTN) The publicly accessible network of analog telephones which enables worldwide communication.

Smart Card Also known as IC (integrated circuit) card. A plastic card containing a memory chip to store information; used mainly for banking.

Speech Recognition Also known as voice recognition. Computer-based process of detecting and identifying spoken words and converting them to written text.

Speech Synthesis The process of emulating human speech by computers. The input is in the form of text which is then transformed to human simulated speech sounds.

Tele-conference Generic term to mean either audio conference or video conference.

Telefax Commonly called facsimile or fax. The transmission of text and graphics in the form of images via telecommunications network.

Teleshopping Also known as homeshopping. A new way of shopping remotely using communications networks whereby the ordering and the payment are made electronically.

Teleworking Use of computers and telecommunications to enable people to work remotely from the office. The substitution of telecommunications for transportation.

Translator A person who translates a written message in one natural language into a written message in another.

Universal Personal Telecommunications (UPT) Location independent telecommunications services based around the concept that an individual user has a permanent number at which he or she can be contacted.

Video Conference Audio-visual interconnection which allows individuals in separate locations to see and talk to one another.

Virtual Private Network (VPN) A logical closed user group among standard connections to the public telephone network or ISDN which provides special services as if dedicated leased lines were used.

Virtual Reality (VR) A technology which provides an interactive interface between human and computer that involves using multiple senses, typically hearing, vision and touch in the computer generated environment.

Voice Mail A telecommunications service enabling electronic storage and delivery of voice messages.

World Wide Web Also known as WWW or Web. A distributed hypermedia system which enables information on the Internet to be accessed via hypertext format.

References

Adams, D. (1979) *The Hitch Hiker's Guide to the Galaxy* . London: Pan Books.

Auckerman, W. (1994) Bilingual and English-language databases in Japan. *Computing Japan* November, 36.

Bekku, S. (1982) *Honyaku wo Manabu [Translation Study]*. Tokyo: Yashio Shuppan.

Bell, R. (1992) Cab computer-speak language: Developing multilingual audio and visual communications systems for transmanche trains. In *Translation and Computer* 14 (pp. 187–96). London: Aslib.

Brand, S. (1988) *The Media Lab: Inventing the Future at MIT*. New York: Penguin Books.

Bright, R (1989) From POTS to VANS. In C. Chang and D. Hitchcock (eds) *The VANS Handbook* (2nd edn). Middlesex: Blenheim Online.

British Telecom World (1989) Fax not friction pp. 33–5.

Clayton, J. (1993) Telecom gets into the TV business. *Dominion*, 17 November, 18.

Communication Week International (1995) Worldwire 6 March, 4.

— (1995) GII nuts and bolts: The supplier view, 20 March, p. 12.

Computing Japan (1994) November, p. 56.

Cunard, J. (1992) Spinning new legal and regulatory webs for telecommunications services in the Pacific: IVANS, Trade Agreements and the Uruguay Round. A paper presented at the Pacific Telecommunications Council '92 conference.

Dertouzos, M. (1991) Communications, computers and networks. *Scientific American*, September, pp. 31–2.

Desmond, E.W. (1995) Can Japan catch the wave? *Time*, 27 February, pp. 41–5.

Dordick, H. (1987) *Information Technology and Economic Growth in NZ*. Wellington: Victoria University Press.

Economist (1994) The age of the thing. 7 January, pp. 29–33.

Elmer-Dewitt, P. (1993) Orgies on-line. *Time*, 31 May, p. 39.

Elmer-Dewitt, P. (1994) Battle for the soul of the Internet. *Time*, 25 July, p. 32.

Enomoto, O. (1988) *Denwa ga Kawaru [Changing Telephone]*. Tokyo: NEC Culture Centre.

Finnie, G. (1994a) The Internet: Life in the fast lane. *CommunicationsWeek International*, 30 May, p. 22.

— (1994b) Companies on Web face an information overload. *CommunicationsWeek International*, 12 December, p. 8.

Fox, B. (1993) Watch out for videophones. *New Scientist*, 6 March, p. 27.

Fraser, N. (1993) The sundial speech understanding and dialogue project: Results and implications for translation. In *Translating and the Computer* 15 (pp. 165–79). London: Aslib.

Gibson, W. (1984) *Neuromancer*. London: Victor Gollancz Ltd.

Gilder, G. (1991) Into the telecosm. *Harvard Business Review*, March-April, pp. 150–3.

Harasim, L. (ed.) (1993) *Global Networks: Computers and International Communication.* Cambridge, MA: MIT Press.

Harrison, H. and Minsky, M. (1993) *The Turing Option.* London: Roc.

Hart, K. (1995) Publishers joining fray. *Communications Week International,* 20 February, p. 24.

Hayes, D. (1994) Global freephone plotted. *Communications Week International,* 17 January, p. 3.

Hovy, E. (1993) MT at your service. *Byte,* January, p. 160.

Japan Times (1992) Translation business special, 21 August.

JEIDA (1992) *Methodology and Criteria on Machine Translation Evaluation,* November. Tokyo: JEIDA.

— (1993) *Research Findings on Utilisation of MT Systems,* April. Tokyo: JEIDA.

Kapor, M. and Weitzner, D. (1993) Social and industrial policy for public networks: Visions for the future. In L. Harasim (ed.) *Global Networks: Computers and International Communication.* Cambridge, MA: MIT Press.

Kline, D. (1995) Align and conquer. *Wired,* February, pp. 110–17.

Kobayashi, K. (1986) *Computers and Communications.* Cambridge, MA: MIT Press.

— (1989) *Rising to the Challenge.* Tokyo: Harcourt Brace Jovanovich Japan.

Langreth, R. (1994) World phone. *Popular Science,* March, pp. 62–3.

Lawson, V. and Vasconcellos, M. (1993) Forty ways to skin a cat: Users report on machine translation. In *Translating and The Computer* 15. London: Aslib.

Lodge, D. (1994) Workshop I Literary translation – Literary panel. In *XIII World Congress of FIT Proceedings: Translation – The Vital Link.* Vol.2. London: Institute of Translation and Interpreting.

Lunde, K. (1993) *Understanding Japanese Information Processing.* Sebastopol, CA: O'Reilly & Associates, Inc.

McLuhan, M. (1967) *The Gutenberg Galaxy.* London: Routledge & Kegan Paul.

Mahon, B. (1990) International (tele)coms: A guide for the faint-hearted. In P. Mayorcas (ed.) *Translating and the Computer* 10. London: Aslib.

Matsumoto, K. and Mukai. K. (1976) *Eigo Tsuyaku eno Michi [The Road to English Interpreter].* Tokyo: Taishukan Shoten.

Morimoto, T. and Kurematsu, A. (1993) Automatic speech translation at ATR. In *MT Summit IV Proceedings.* Tokyo: MT Summit IV Secretariat, Asia-Pacific Association for Machine Translation.

Nagao, M. (1989) *Machine Translation: How Far Can it Go?* (N. Cook, trans.). Oxford: Oxford University Press (Original work published 1986).

— (1992) MT Technology: Its application and future (a keynote speech given at MT Symposium held in Osaka, Japan). In *Kikai Honyaku Sisutemu no Jitsuyouka ni kansuru Chosakekka [Research Findings on Utilisation of MT Systems].* Tokyo: The Japan Electronic Industry Development Association (JEIDA).

— (1993) Machine translation today. In *Denshi Kogyo Geppo [Electronic Industry Monthly]* 35 (10), 10.

New Breeze: Quarterly of the New ITU Association of Japan, Inc. (1993) NTT major growth in distribution of ISDN; Increase to 310,000 by end of March 1994, April, 5 (1), pp. 4–5.

— (1995) MPT issues white paper on information and communications industry for FY 1994, July 7 (3), 8.

Newmark, P. (1993) *Paragraphs on Translation.* Clevedon: Multilingual Matters Ltd.

Nida, E. and Taber, C. (1969) *The Theory and Practice of Translation*. Leiden: E.J. Brill.

Nikkei Datapuro/OA Sokuho [Nikkei Data Professional/ OA News Bulletin] (1990) December, 2.

Nirenburg, S. Carbonell, J. Tomita, M. and Goodman, K. (1992) *Machine Translation: A Knowledge-Based Approach*. San Mateo, CA: Morgan-Kaufmann.

NTT Gijutsu Doko Kenkyukai [NTT Technology Trend Group]. (1990) *2005 nen no johotsuushin gijutsu* [*Information and telecommunications technologies in 2005*]. Tokyo: NTT Shupan.

NZ ISDN Forum (1993).

Obenaus, G. (1993) The Internet – An electronic treasure trove. In *Translating and the Computer* 15. London: Aslib.

OECD (Organization for Economic Co-operation and Development) (1992) *Telecommunications and Broadcasting: Convergence or Collision?* (1992) Paris: OECD.

Poster, M. (1991) *Joho Yoshiki Ron* [*The Mode of Information*] (H. Muroi and H. Yoshioka, trans.). Tokyo: Iwanami Shoten (Original work published 1990).

Qian, H. (1993) Telephone translation. In *XIII World Congress of FIT Proceedings Translation – The Vital Link*. Vol.1 (pp. 433–39). London: Institute of Translation and Interpreting.

Quarterman, J. (1993) The global matrix of minds. In L. Harasim (ed.) *Global Networks: Computers and International Communication*. Cambridge, MA: MIT Press.

Rheingold, H. (1993) Is the Info Superhighway headed the wrong way? *International BusinessWeek*, 20 December, p. 7.

Robinson, P. (1991) Globalization, telecommunications and trade. *Futures* 23, 801–14.

Sager, J. (1990) Ten years of machine translation design and application: From FAHQT to realism. In P. Mayorcas (ed.) *Translating and the Computer* 10. London: Aslib.

Sakamoto, M. and Itagaki, S. (1993) Translator shortages, translation shortcomings. *Pacific Friend* 20 (20) March, 7.

Schank, R. and Kass, A. (1988) Knowledge representation in people and machine. In U. Eco, M. Santambrogio and P. Violi (eds) *Meaning and Mental Representations*. Bloomington: Indiana University press.

Scheresse, F. (1992) Systran: Or the reality of machine translation. In *Translating and the Computer* 13. London: Aslib.

Shapard, J. (1993) Language, character codes and electronic isolation in Japan. In L. Harasim (ed.) *Global Networks: Computers and International Communication*. Cambridge, MA: MIT Press.

Smith, M. (1987) A matter of interpretation (translation's role in international relations). *Newsweek*, 14 December, (p. 9).

Steiner, G. (1992) *After Babel: Aspects of Language & Translation* (p. xvii). London, New York: Oxford University Press.

Stentiford, F. and Steer, M. (1988) Machine translation of speech. *British Telecom Journal*, April, p. 6.

Stewart, T. (1993) Welcome to the revolution. *Fortune*, 13 December, p. 2–11.

Suzuki, S. (1993) IN rollout in Japan, *IEEE Communications Magazine*, March, p. 54.

Telecom Corporation of New Zealand Limited 1995 Annual Report.

Telecomeuropa's ISDN Newsletter (1994), 18 April, p. 10.

Tiffin, J. (1990a) Translation process according to the domain theory of communi-
cation. Unpublished manuscript.
— (1990b) Advancing the nation. *Supplementary Proceedings of Telecommunications
Users Association of New Zealand [TUANZ] Conference.* Auckland: TUANZ.
Time (1993) 13 September. From the Publisher.
— (1994) 10 January. To Our Readers.
TUANZ Towards 2000 (1993) *Proceedings of Telecommunications Users Association of
New Zealand [TUANZ] Conference* . Auckland: TUANZ.
Valverde, E. (1990) *Language for Export.* Canberra: Office of Multicultural Affairs.
Vasconcellos, M. (1993a) Machine translation. *Byte*, January, p. 156.
— (1993b) The present state of machine translation usage technology or: How do I
use thee? Let me count the ways. In *MT Summit IV Proceedings.* Tokyo: MT
Summit IV Secretariat, Asia-Pacific Association for Machine Translation.
Wahlster, W. (1993) Verbmobil: Translation of face-to-face dialogs. In *MT Summit
IV Proceedings* (pp. 127–35), Tokyo: MT Summit IV Secretariat, Asia-Pacific
Association for Machine Translation.
Walsh, J. (1992) World's fair videophone. *Teleconference*, 10 (6), 27.
West, M. (1992) *The Ringmaster.* London: Mandarin Paperbacks.
Wilkinson, E. (1983) *Japan versus Europe: A History of Misunderstanding.* Penguin
Books.
Wired (1994) May, p. 26.
Woolley, B. (1992) *Virtual Worlds.* Penguin Books.

Index